TITLES IN THE SERIES

The Development of Western Civilization

*Narrative Essays in the History of Our Tradition from
Its Origins in Ancient Israel and Greece to the Present*

Edited by Edward W. Fox
*Professor of Modern European History
Cornell University*

THE

Mediaeval Church

MARSHALL W. BALDWIN

NEW YORK UNIVERSITY

Cornell University Press

ITHACA, NEW YORK

Copyright 1953 by Cornell University

CORNELL UNIVERSITY PRESS

First published 1953
Second printing 1955
Third printing 1956
Fourth printing 1958
Fifth printing 1959
Sixth printing 1960
Seventh printing 1962
Eighth printing 1963
Ninth printing 1964
Tenth printing 1965
Eleventh printing 1965
Twelfth printing 1967

PRINTED IN THE UNITED STATES OF AMERICA

BY VAIL-BALLOU PRESS, INC.

Foreword

THE proposition that each generation must rewrite history is more widely quoted than practiced. In the field of college texts on western civilization, the conventional accounts have been revised, and sources and supplementary materials have been developed; but it is too long a time since the basic narrative has been rewritten to meet the rapidly changing needs of new college generations. In the mid-twentieth century such an account must be brief, well written, and based on unquestioned scholarship and must assume almost no previous historical knowledge on the part of the reader. It must provide a coherent analysis of the development of western civilization and its basic values. It must, in short, constitute a systematic introduction to the collective memory of that tradition which we are being asked to defend. This series of narrative essays was undertaken in an effort to provide such a text for an introductory history survey course and is being published in the present form in the belief that the requirements of that one course reflected a need that is coming to be widely recognized.

Now that the classic languages, the Bible, the great historical novels, even most non-American history, have dropped out of the normal college preparatory program, it is imperative that a text in the history of European civilization be fully self-explanatory. This means not only that it must begin at the beginning, with the origins of our civilization in ancient Israel and Greece, but that it must introduce every name or event that takes an integral place in the account and ruthlessly delete all others no matter how firmly imbedded in historical protocol. Only thus simplified and complete will the narrative present a sufficiently clear outline of those major trends and developments that have led from the beginning of our recorded time to the most pressing of our current problems. This simplification, however, need not involve intellectual dilution or evasion. On the contrary, it can effectively raise rather than lower the level of presentation. It is on this assumption that the present series has been based, and each contributor has been urged to write for a mature and literate audience. It is hoped, therefore, that the essays may also prove profitable and rewarding to readers outside the college classroom.

The plan of the first part of the series is to sketch, in related essays, the narrative of our history from its origins to the eve of the French Revolution; each is to be written by a recognized scholar and is designed to serve as the basic reading for one week in a semester course. The developments of the nineteenth and twentieth centuries will be covered in a succeeding series which will provide the same quantity of reading material for each week of the second semester. This scale of presentation has been adopted in the conviction that any understanding of the central problem of the preservation of the integrity and dignity of the individual human being depends first on an examination of the origins of our tradition in the politics and philosophy of the ancient Greeks and the religion of the ancient Hebrews and then on a relatively more detailed knowledge of its recent development within our industrial urban society.

The decision to devote equal space to twenty-five centuries and to a century and a half was based on analogy with the human memory. Those events most remote tend to be remembered in least detail but often with a sense of clarity and perspective that is absent in more recent and more crowded recollections. If the roots of our tradition must be identified, their relation to the present must be carefully developed. The nearer the narrative approaches contemporary times, the more difficult and complicated this becomes. Recent experience must be worked over more carefully and in more detail if it is to contribute effectively to an understanding of the contemporary world.

It may be objected that the series attempts too much. The attempt is being made, however, on the assumption that any historical development should be susceptible of meaningful treatment on any scale and in the realization that a very large proportion of today's college students do not have more time to invest in this part of their education. The practical alternative appears to lie between some attempt to create a new brief account of the history of our tradition and the abandonment of any serious effort to communicate the essence of that tradition to all but a handful of our students. It is the conviction of everyone contributing to this series that the second alternative must not be accepted by default.

In a series covering such a vast sweep of time, few scholars would find themselves thoroughly at home in the fields covered by more than one or two of the essays. This means, in practice, that almost every essay should be written by a different author. In spite of apparent drawbacks, this procedure promises real advantages. Each contributor will be in a position to set higher standards of accuracy and insight in an essay encompassing a major portion of the field of his life's work than could ordinarily be expected in surveys of some ten or twenty centuries. The inevitable discontinuity of style and interpretation could be modified by editorial coordination; but it was felt that some discontinuity was in itself desirable. No illusion is more easily acquired by the student in an elementary course, or is more prejudicial to the efficacy of such a course, than that a single smoothly articulated text represents the very substance of history itself. If the shift from author to author, week by week, raises difficulties for the beginning student, they are difficulties that will not so much impede his progress as contribute to his growth.

In this essay, *The Mediaeval Church*, Mr. Marshall W. Baldwin presents his subject not merely as a political organization immersed in a struggle for temporal power, but rather as an all-pervasive aspect of mediaeval life itself. The papacy was no more the church than the empire was feudalism. The church was Christendom, and Christendom was the totality of European society. It was a way of life which had for its first purpose the worship of God and after that the salvation and civilization of man. Its members were the inhabitants of western Europe led and comforted by their parish priests, ruled and—according to chance—abused or protected by their lords and bishops, who all together glimpsed only occasionally and from afar the passing might and splendor of emperors and popes. It is this church which Professor Baldwin has described with a skill and accuracy grounded in historical discipline and with a sympathy and understanding derived from religious faith.

EDWARD WHITING FOX

Ithaca, New York
August, 1953

Contents

Introduction

THE mediaeval Christian church embraced in its membership virtually all inhabitants of Europe. The occasional Jews, Moslems, and dissenters, or heretics, who appeared and reappeared were the only exceptions. Europe was, therefore, Christendom. Its society was formed by religion to an extent never equaled in any other epoch of its history; and as a result, an inextricable association of things religious and secular developed. From this interweaving of the ecclesiastical with the political arose the tendency of modern historians to overemphasize what might be called the external history of the church, its manifold dealings with secular states. Although such developments are an essential part of the fabric of European history, they do not constitute the most important element in the mission and therefore the history of the church.

Briefly stated, the church's primary purpose, its *raison d'être*, embodies two fundamental things, each closely related to the other. First, there is the solemn public worship of God, the homage which man owes his Creator. It is for this reason that monks renounce the world for a life of prayer. It is to this end that the church has elaborated what is called the liturgy. Liturgy is a word of Greek derivation

meaning service and signifies the order of prayer and ceremony which constitutes Christian worship.

A second objective, actually inseparable from the first, is
the sanctification of individual souls, a continuous process
whereby men grow spiritually in a manner different from,
but analogous to, physical growth. Thus, mediaeval theologians who did so much to establish and define the terminology of Christianity spoke of man's supernatural life, the
life of the soul above the natural life of the body.

Especially important in this spiritual growth and the salvation of souls were certain specific ceremonies called sacraments. Mediaeval theologians also did much to clarify the
church's teaching concerning the sacraments and to give
them explicit definition. The accepted number came to be
seven: baptism, the Eucharist or, as it was popularly called,
the Mass, penance, confirmation, holy orders, marriage, and
extreme unction. These will be discussed more fully in later
pages.

To sum up, the church taught that each human person was
destined for an eternal life after death and that he might accomplish much during his earthly existence to prepare himself for heaven by nourishing his supernatural life. He must
acknowledge his Creator in worship and accept the means
offered for his sanctification. Should he of his own free will
fall from grace, he could expect punishment, temporary in a
state called purgatory if he were penitent, permanent if he
finally rejected his Creator.

In addition to these initial reflections on the church's mission, the student may profitably consider what the mediaeval
church was not. Above all, it was not an institution dedicated primarily to the cause of social reform. It was interested
in individual souls. Society mattered only insofar as it aided

or impeded individual sanctification. If society were to be changed or improved, this could be done only by changing or improving the individuals who composed it. The church, therefore, did not condemn feudalism or serfdom, although it did oppose excesses. If it endeavored to follow its Founder's precepts in protecting the weak, the sick, and the poor, it was also solicitous for the souls of the wealthy and the strong. Moreover, the action of the church on society varied tremendously with conditions and with individuals. Some ecclesiastics were exceptionally active in promoting what would today be termed charitable enterprises. Others were neglectful or apathetic. Both groups, however, would have regarded such activities as secondary in importance, their spiritual value measured by the extent to which they were dedicated to God.

The historian cannot, therefore, relate the purely secular history of the church without allowing fundamental matters to escape him. He may judge a temporal kingdom by the manner in which it promotes the welfare of its subjects. But spiritual welfare is not merely difficult, it is all but impossible to appraise by normal historical evidence and methods. Accordingly, in describing the many controversies between churchmen and statesmen which fill the pages of mediaeval history, he must remember that such terms as "triumph" and "decline" can easily be misleading. A pope may emerge "victorious" from an altercation with an emperor and the church gain no spiritual strength, just as a political defeat could be a spiritual triumph.

By the year 900 the familiar ecclesiastical organization of priests and bishops under the headship of the bishop of Rome had extended its jurisdiction over a fairly large area of western Europe and had begun to push eastward and southward beyond the frontiers of the old Carolingian empire. Monasticism was now an accepted and widespread form of religious life. And a regular clergy, as the monks were called, had been added to the ordinary or secular clergy of parish and town.

During the tenth century Christianity in eastern Europe, the area of Byzantine influence, also expanded as territory was recovered from the Moslems or as the faith was carried to Balkan and Slavic peoples. Relations between Rome and Constantinople had been strained in the ninth century, but no permanent rift had developed and the entire church remained united under the pope. Only certain heretical groups of oriental Christians were actually separated. Yet it remains true that Byzantine ecclesiastical history, like Byzantine political history, unfolded under conditions markedly different from those which affected the West. It is, therefore, to the West that we shall turn first, later resuming the story of the relations between eastern and western Christianity.

CHAPTER I

The Western Church
in the Feudal Age

THE period roughly included between the years 900 and
1150 was predominantly feudal, and feudalism, it will be recalled, developed to meet certain adverse conditions—weak
central government, limited commerce, invasion.[1] Since
feudalism implied decentralization, life tended to become
localized. Communications were inadequate. Violence and
insecurity were common. As a consequence, orderly ecclesiastical administration—and the same was true of secular
government—was gravely endangered. All this threw a
heavy responsibility upon ecclesiastical individuals, for their
duties had all too often to be fulfilled in isolation.

Another feature of feudalism which is pertinent to this
discussion is the widespread private appropriation of what
had once been public authority. As the functions of government became decentralized, the material support—usually land—on which government rested tended to fall into
the hands of the individuals immediately concerned. With
this process went the dependence of lesser persons upon the
more wealthy and powerful. An analogous development
took place with ecclesiastical government and property. In

[1] Sidney Painter, *Mediaeval Society* (Ithaca, N.Y., 1951).

addition, ecclesiastical endowments were often leased out to or appropriated by laymen. By the tenth century, therefore, the considerable properties of the church were by no means under the exclusive control of churchmen. This was true of small properties as well as large. Indeed, it was particularly true of the parish priest, and with his problems our discussion will open.

The Parish Priest

The smallest unit in the ecclesiastical establishment was the parish. Actually, the term "parish" was originally used to designate the jurisdiction of a bishop. But in the course of time it has been associated with the area served by the priest, and it is in this sense that it will be used here. In the feudal age most parishes were rural, for towns were neither numerous nor populous. The parishioners, therefore, were predominantly peasant folk who lived under the dominion of a *seigneur*, usually a layman, but occasionally a bishop or an abbot.

Like so many institutions in the Middle Ages, parishes differed not only in size but in function. There were, for example, "baptismal churches" (*ecclesiae baptismales*), distinguished by the possession of the baptismal font. This permitted the administration of the essential and first sacrament of baptism, which removed the stain of original sin and made the new Christian a "child of God." Certain lesser churches which did not possess this privilege might nonetheless be designated parishes. There were also rural chapels, oratories, and the like, sometimes served by clerics dependent on a baptismal church.

The system of rural parishes had originally been established by the bishops in the early Middle Ages and had been adjusted to meet the religious needs of existing villages or the great landed estates (*villas*). They were endowed with property for their support and for the assistance of the local poor. Endowments increased with gifts from the faithful. Moreover, very early in ecclesiastical history the tithe, or tenth, was expected from the local population. At first the tithe was a voluntary contribution, but in the Carolingian period it became compulsory.

During the Carolingian and post-Carolingian periods, many—perhaps the great majority—of the rural church properties and revenues fell under the control of local magnates. Such a magnate might be a bishop, in which case the priest came under his jurisdiction in two capacities. The bishop was, first of all, the ecclesiastical superior of the priest. But he was also the suzerain from whom the priest held the parish property. Further, despite the opposition of certain church authorities, parishes also came under the jurisdiction of monasteries. If such were the case, the parish duties might be performed by monastic clergy delegated for the purpose.

The extent to which church property became feudalized varied greatly. Conditions in Italy were unlike those in Frankish Gaul or in early mediaeval Germany. In the following paragraphs, therefore, an attempt will be made to describe an "average" parish situation. The student must remember that no set of conditions in mediaeval times can be designated as absolutely typical.

Certain it was, however, that upon the shoulders of the parish priest fell the immediate responsibility for the spiritual welfare of the local population. He was, to use a term current in later years, the *curé* (Latin *curare*, to care for), because his was the care of souls. The sacraments which intimately affected the lives of his parishioners it was his duty to administer. As we have indicated, these included the first and necessary sacrament of baptism. Then, to those who fell into serious sin after baptism there was available the sacrament of penance. The penitent who was sincerely contrite was expected to confess his sins orally, but privately, to the priest, who then pronounced the words of absolution imparting God's forgiveness. For the priest was a custodian of Christ's commission to his apostles. "Whose sins you shall forgive, they are forgiven them; and whose sins you shall retain, they are retained" (John 20:21–22). Thus was removed both the guilt of the sin and the eternal punishment. Though God's mercy might restore the sinner, his justice required a "satisfaction." This indebtedness must be met either in this world or in the next. Accordingly, the priest enjoined a "penance," some act of a religious nature. In the Middle Ages penances, especially for serious crimes, were often severe. A long fast, even a distant pilgrimage, might be required. To guide the parish priest there appeared manuals called penitentials which specified the proper penances.

The church also taught that for those whose satisfaction of divine justice was incomplete at the time of their death— and this would apply to all except the saints—there was a temporal state called purgatory wherein some sort of suffering fulfilled the remaining debt. Souls in purgatory, however, could be aided by the prayers of the faithful on earth; and further, the truly penitent might hope for the remission of all or part of their purgation by obtaining what was called an indulgence. Granted by ecclesiastical authority, this remission was believed to draw on the superabundant merits of Christ and the saints and to be grounded in His promise, as recorded by Matthew (18:18) "Whatsoever thou shalt bind upon earth it shall be bound also in heaven; and whatsoever thou shalt loose on earth, it shall be loosed also in heaven."

It was not in the power of the parish priest to grant an indulgence. That was for higher authority, although the priest might instruct his parishioners in the manner of obtaining indulgences. Notwithstanding, the vital significance of the sacrament of penance in the scheme of salvation enhanced the importance of the priest in society. Indeed, the power to administer the sacraments goes far to explain the paramount influence of the clergy in the mediaeval world.

For persons critically ill there was a special sacrament called extreme unction, actually an anointing of someone in danger of death. In the Middle Ages the dead were commonly buried in the graveyard adjacent to the parish church, a custom which survived until the advent of modern populous cities necessitated cemeteries in the suburbs.

Especially important in the scheme of both worship and salvation was the sacrament known formally as Holy Eucharist and popularly as the Mass.[2] Mediaeval Christians believed that when a priest repeated Christ's words "This is My Body, and this is My Blood" over bread and wine he was not only commemorating Christ's "last supper" with His apostles, but that the bread and wine were miraculously changed into the Body and Blood of Christ. Theologians described this as "transubstantiation," a term which may confuse the modern student because substance (*substantia*) did not necessarily signify something material and tangible. That is to say, the doctrine was not subject to verification by ordinary human observation since it made no claim that

[2] From words spoken by the priest at the end of the Mass: "Ite, missa est," or "Go, it is the dismissal."

the bread and wine changed their physical appearance.

Theologians also taught that when the priest offered the consecrated bread and wine at the altar during the ceremony of the Mass he was continuing the sacrifice of Christ on the cross. The Mass accordingly was a sacrifice prefigured in the ceremonial sense in ancient Hebrew ritual. As such it required an altar, and the altar always occupied the most prominent place in the church building.

The performance of the Mass was, of course, restricted to members of the ordained clergy, a fact which immensely enhanced their importance in mediaeval society. But the laity participated actively by their presence and, provided they were not in a state of serious sin, by consuming a portion of the consecrated elements. This was called Holy Communion. During the Middle Ages it became customary in the West, for reasons of convenience and to avoid sacrilege, for laymen to receive only the consecrated bread. This did not mean an imperfect reception of Holy Communion, for it was held that Christ was present entirely in either the bread or the wine. Communion under both species continues in the East and is still the rule in oriental churches.

Living as he did close to the village people, a parish priest had many opportunities for devoted service. It was his duty, for example, to allocate a portion of his revenues to the poor. And his advice must have been frequently sought in many parochial matters. If he were competent to do so—and this was unfortunately rare in the early Middle Ages—he gave some rudimentary instruction to village children, perhaps to boys who gave promise of becoming priests themselves. But he was also subject to many temptations from which priests in a less turbulent age are immune. He was surrounded by an illiterate and superstitious population prone to attribute all its fortunes and misfortunes to direct angelic or diabolic intervention. Nobles may have been somewhat more refined, but more educated usually only in a military or governmental sense. The priest's own education was of the scantiest, and, at least in the period before 1100, his opportunities for self-improvement were rare. As a consequence, it is not surprising that evidence of clerical shortcomings abounds in the decrees of ecclesiastical councils and in what records there are of episcopal visitations.

To counteract the dangers of clerical isolation, the church authorities encouraged the practice whereby a group of priests lived together in a common religious life. This corporate semimonastic existence was rare in the early Middle Ages; although more often a feature of town religious organization, it was occasionally found in rural areas.

Most evidence of lapses from a proper standard of conduct is in effect negative; official criticism is always directed at offenders. The priest who fulfilled his duties with zeal is mentioned only in those rare instances in which he rose in the church's hierarchy, became famous, and was the subject of a biography. If many devoted parish priests lived obscure lives, it cannot be said that their work went entirely unappreciated. Although written in the later Middle Ages, the description of the priest in Chaucer's *Prologue* is such a classic that it may be quoted here.

> A good man was ther of religioun,
> And was a povre Persoun of a toun;
> But riche he was of holy thoght and werk.
> He was also a learned man a clerk,
> That Cristes gospel trewely wolde preche;

His parisshens devoutly would he teche;
Benigne he was, and wonder diligent,
And in adversitee ful pacient.[3]

A unit in the ecclesiastical order, the country parish was
also, in a material sense, a unit in the feudal order. Nowhere
was that typically mediaeval amalgam of the spiritual and
the temporal more evident than in the position of the rural
parish priest. Like the cathedral or the abbey, only on a
smaller scale, the parish was a piece of property. The church
building was often a simple, even a rude, structure of wood.
Stone churches came into style as the Middle Ages pro-
gressed into the eleventh and twelfth centuries, but were
rare in the early period. The parish also possessed an appropriate amount of land. According to ancient regulations, this
was at least a *mansis*, the small agricultural unit within the
villa or manorial estate. Sometimes a minimum of four serfs
was included. Often, however, the property was increased
by pious donations.

In addition to real property, certain revenues were due
the parish; and ancient custom, repeatedly set forth in con-
ciliar decrees, had long established the tithe or tenth as a
normally required contribution of the parish population. It
might be paid in money or in kind, depending on circumstances. Further, many oblations or offerings, originally
voluntary, had, despite regulations to the contrary, become
virtually compulsory. Such, for example, were "contributions" for sacraments.

With this revenue, the priest was expected to keep his
church in repair, provide for the proper celebration of the
liturgy, make certain payments to his bishop, give a portion
to the poor, and maintain himself and, if he had any, his

[3] W. W. Skeat, ed., *The Student's Chaucer* (Oxford, 1927), p. 425.

assistants. According to early mediaeval canon law, the tithe, though ultimately the property of the bishop, was to be divided into quarters of which one went to the bishop, one to the poor, another for the fabric of the church, and the last for the needs of the priest.

The parish, though dedicated to a patron saint and regarded as his patrimony, often formed part of the domain of a feudal lord. As a consequence, the material assets of a parish were not usually at the exclusive disposal of the priest. Indeed, the term "seigneur of the parish" was in use in France down to the Revolution. The justification for this seigneurial authority lay in the fact that the lord, or his ancestors, had founded the parish. Many parishes, originally founded and endowed by Carolingian monarchs, were later parceled out to various magnates just as were fiefs. So common was this practice that ecclesiastical authorities, at least in some instances, regarded it as normal and legal. In somewhat the same way, certain parishes were established by or fell under the domination of a monastery or bishop.

Thus it was that the priest, who within the organization of the church was subject to the bishop, actually had to demonstrate his allegiance to a seigneur. The latter—who might, of course, be a bishop or an abbot—officially installed him in his parish and probably also had had something to say about his nomination to the office. In addition, some bishops interpreted canon law as giving them disposition of the parish tithes. So also did certain monasteries. Offerings were even appropriated by seigneurs. Finally, this disintegration of parochial assets reached a point where a specific portion of the revenue, the *presbyteratus*, was allocated to the priest by his seigneur. The parish had become a fief.

Priests in Towns

Although towns were not as populous or as numerous as in the latter Middle Ages, there were many instances of significant urban life by the eleventh century. In some of the larger city parishes, a number of priests led a semimonastic life under a rule. Because these communities were called *collegia*, such a large church was called a collegiate church. The life of a priest in a collegiate church was very different from that of his confrère in the country. His parochial problems were different, and his opportunities for education and advancement were more numerous. Priests in large churches were expected to chant the offices, as the liturgical services were called, at the appointed hours much as did monks in cloisters. The great feast days, much more frequent than in modern times, required a solemn celebration of the liturgy, sometimes of considerable duration.

The duty of publicly chanting the liturgy also devolved upon the priests attached to a cathedral church, the church of a bishop. These priests, originally chosen by the bishop, were known as canons, and their corporate organization, the chapter, was headed by a dignitary of their own choosing, usually the dean or the provost. As a body of chanters they were also called the *schola cantorum*, and the leader in the chant was the precentor (*praecantor*). Some cathedrals had as many as sixty or seventy canons, though most chapters were much smaller. Moreover, although some chapters were actually monastic establishments, most seem to have been composed of secular (that is, nonmonastic) canons, who nevertheless lived under a kind of monastic rule traditionally ascribed to St. Augustine, the celebrated bishop of Hippo and great ecclesiastical authority of late Roman times.

In addition to their liturgical duties, the cathedral canons in most instances elected the bishop, a function which added considerably to their importance. From his funds the bishop provided for their maintenance an amount at one time carefully determined and known as the *praebenda*. In the course of time, cathedral chapters received many donations and, after the eleventh century, exemptions and privileges which made them almost independent of the bishop. Moreover, *praebenda* sometimes became individualized, and canons receiving their share took meals outside the common refectory. Eventually, the term "prebend" signified the "living" of a canon, much as the feudal term "benefice" might be used to designate the "living" of a parish priest. Prebends too were feudalized, the gift of laymen as well as of ecclesiastics.[4]

The Bishop

Bishops stood at the summit of the ecclesiastical hierarchy because bishops were in the mind of the church the successors of Christ's apostles. The prospective candidate for the episcopate became a bishop through the sacrament of holy orders. The most solemn moment in the bishop's consecration was when three other bishops placed their hands on the candidate's head and pronounced the words, "Receive the Holy Spirit (*Accipe Sanctum Spiritum*)." Only a bishop could confer holy orders on a priest. Even the supremacy of the pope rested on the fact that he was bishop of Rome, a see founded by St. Peter, chief of the apostles.

[4] It is an interesting fact that much of the terminology of mediaeval Christianity survived in the post-Reformation Anglican church. Students of English literature, and especially of the novels of Anthony Trollope, will be familiar with such terms as precentor, dean, vicar, canon, archdeacon, and the like.

The area of a bishop's jurisdiction was called, in the tenth and eleventh centuries, an *episcopatus*. Later, the terms *parochia* and "diocese" came into general use, and the latter has lasted. At the center of the diocese, to use the word which has become familiar, was the city (French *cité*) where the bishop resided. In the lands that once formed a part of the Roman Empire, the episcopal sees were actually communities which had been centers of a Roman *civitas*. Many of them ceased to be important commercially or politically, no longer cities in the modern sense of the word. Notwithstanding, the city was almost always the seat of a bishop and his cathedral church.

Some episcopal sees disappeared during the invasions. Others were amalgamated, and by the eleventh century many new sees had been established in newly occupied frontier lands. Canterbury in England and Magdeburg in what was then eastern Germany are examples. All such changes or new establishments were carried out during the Carolingian era by mutual arrangements on the part of the pope, neighboring bishops, and local princes. Despite the weakness of actual papal power in that period, it was always held that no see could be created or suppressed without the pope's consent.

The bishop was responsible for the orderly performance of all ecclesiastical functions within his diocese. The immediate concerns of the cathedral church and the city were in the hands of the cathedral chapter. And, as was pointed out, the canons under their dean or provost were often a semiautonomous body. Nevertheless, ultimate authority and, therefore, responsibility rested with the bishop. If, for example, the cathedral needed repair or a new one was to be built, the bishop must take the initiative. Indeed, many bishops were noted as builders, and architecture is the richer for their efforts.

Bishops were required to inspect periodically the parishes throughout their dioceses in order to maintain discipline and settle any matters which lay beyond the local priest's competence. It would be a bishop's duty, for example, to administer the sacrament of confirmation. This sacrament, like baptism received only once, conferred on a Christian soul a special strengthening grace. A bishop was also obliged to hold at least once a year in his cathedral city a synod or meeting of his diocesan clergy. All parish priests were expected to attend. Furthermore, although many monastic communities were exempt from episcopal jurisdiction, as will presently be explained, those which were not had to be visited and regulated by the bishop. Finally, only a bishop could administer the sacrament of holy orders to prospective candidates for the priesthood.

The bishop also had to maintain a court for the settlement of diocesan litigation. In the Middle Ages, litigation between ecclesiastical persons and communities or disputes involving religious matters in which lay people were concerned fell under the jurisdiction of canon or church law. The bishop's court was normally the court of first instance for such controversies, and the vast majority of cases were settled there, although appeals to Rome increased markedly.

To assist him in his manifold activities, the bishop had certain diocesan functionaries of whom the archdeacons were the most important. Archdeacons, usually priests, were often of great assistance to their bishops, and some exercised considerable influence on policy. A somewhat special example was the monk, Hildebrand, who as archdeacon of Rome strongly influenced the activities of the see over which he later presided as pope. Occasionally an archdeacon held court or presided over the bishop's court. In a few instances a kind of rivalry developed between bishop and archdeacons.

A bishop's immediate superior was the archbishop. An archbishop, or metropolitan as he was sometimes called, was a bishop whose see was an important city, a metropolis, and whose archdiocese or province included the more limited territorial jurisdictions of other bishops. His functions, therefore, were those of an ordinary bishop on a slightly larger scale. He held archdiocesan synods which all bishops within his jurisdiction attended.

Finally, all bishops and archbishops were obliged to visit Rome. Irregular in the early Middle Ages, these official episcopal visits were by the eleventh century required periodically. Moreover, presence at Rome might also be demanded for a special occasion, such as an ecumenical or general council of bishops with the pope.

Exacting as were a bishop's ecclesiastical obligations, they were not, in the Middle Ages, his sole concern, for bishops had many temporal responsibilities as well. His church was the center of a domain which, in addition to dwellings for himself and his clergy, comprised manors, vineyards, and even fiscal rights such as income from tolls. All this, the *res ecclesiae*, was held to be not secular property, but the patrimony of the patron saint. Actually, of course, the bishop administered this collection of properties, privileges, and responsibilities. Thus he became identified with the bishopric, much as the count, originally a royal functionary, became identified with the county.

Various concessions by kings who granted immunities, tolls, or customs rights, occasionally even the right of coinage, furthered this secularization of the bishopric. Moreover, as the power of the king's official, normally the count, was thus diminished, the judicial responsibility of the bishop within his diocese was enhanced. In certain cases, bishops were given political authority over all or part of a county. Such a policy appealed particularly to the kings of Germany. Since no one could legitimately inherit the bishop's authority, German rulers fortified the secular power of bishops as a counterweight to the great lay feudatories. In short, the bishopric, like the county, gradually took its position in the feudal hierarchy.

The consequences of feudalism for the bishopric are clear. As a lord and administrator of landed property, the bishop had to supervise the affairs of his own vassals. Much of this could be delegated to subordinates, but the ultimate responsibility was his. As a vassal the bishop was expected to take an oath of allegiance, homage commonly not being required of an ecclesiastic. He must supply men-at-arms and attend the feudal court. Indeed, certain rulers demanded that bishops appear with their feudal military levy in person.

To a conscientious cleric, anxious to fulfill his churchly duties, these obligations must have seemed a real burden, as indeed they were. But to some, attendance at a king's court was exciting, a welcome break in the routine of ecclesiastical activity. Such, no doubt, must have been the attitude of the more worldly bishops, especially those who had entered the church, or been forced to enter by ambitious relatives, in the hope of social or political advancement. The prospective revenues of a wealthy bishopric could be a source of temptation to a feudal family oversupplied with younger sons. And simony, the purchase or sale of ecclesiastical preferment, was unfortunately not uncommon in the tenth and eleventh centuries.

Such considerations go far toward explaining why a number of bishops—enough to have attracted the attention of contemporary chroniclers—behaved, after their installment, with something less than episcopal dignity. An extreme case, which caused one of the great scandals of the early Middle Ages, was the bishop who was so inordinately fond of hunting that he moved the altar and furnishings to the porch of his church and stabled his horses and dogs in the nave. Happily such cases were rare. More common were the bishops who interpreted their feudal military obligation in a literal manner. Some, deferring to the canonical injunction which forbids any cleric to shed blood, swung a heavy mace. Others were less squeamish. In general, society condoned such activities, especially during engagements with the infidel. It is no coincidence that Archbishop Turpin, who in the *Song of Roland* laid about him among the Moslems with signal and sanguinary effect, was one of the most popular of mediaeval heroes.

Because a bishop's position in the ecclesiastical hierarchy was so important and because he was, in effect, a political functionary as well, the choice of bishops was a significant matter. In fact, episcopal elections have repeatedly figured in controversies both within the church and between the church and lay rulers. Ancient custom, embodied in canon law, decreed an election by clergy and people (*electio cleri et populi*). But this did not signify any definite system of voting in the modern sense. *Electio* meant choice. Actually, the role of the people was ordinarily reduced to the acclamation of a candidate chosen by the clergy, perhaps in conjunction with the magnates of the region. Normally, therefore, the preponderant part in electing a bishop fell to the clergy and, by the tenth century, usually the canons of the cathedral.

In practice, temporal princes frequently presented their candidates whom the local clergy and people were expected to accept. This practice seems to have originated in the Carolingian period when the king—and this was particularly true of Charlemagne—as the "protector" of the church granted permission for an election to be held. Procedures which developed under Charlemagne continued in the several sections into which the Carolingian empire divided. A prince of good will might concede free elections, and a number of diplomas so stipulating were granted by princes and kings. In general, however, temporal rulers reserved the right of confirming the nominee. A refusal ordinarily meant that the prince then proceeded to choose his own candidate. In one way or another, the kings of France and Germany habitually intervened in episcopal elections, especially after the middle of the tenth century. One of the consequences was the predominance of noble-born men among the higher clergy.

Once elected, either canonically by the cathedral chapter or as a consequence of princely intervention, the nominee had still to be confirmed and consecrated by other bishops, normally under the auspices of the metropolitan. The bishops of the province assembled in synod, examined the candidate, and then proceeded to the solemn ceremony of consecration. Since an examination could prove unsatisfactory, it was possible for an archbishop to exercise a veto on an episcopal election. Certain metropolitans in the ninth and tenth centuries sought in this and other ways to exalt their authority in defiance of the prevailing influence of local princes and even, in some cases, against the pope. But these pretensions to independence were not successful. Most metropolitans accepted episcopal candidates even when presented by princes.

There remained the rights reserved to Rome, for the bishop of Rome, or the pope, as he had come to be called, was the supreme head of the church. This headship rested on the primitive doctrine of Petrine supremacy: that Christ had singled out St. Peter as the chief of his apostles, that Peter had visited and founded his see at Rome, and that the bishops of Rome were his successors. The full constitutional significance of papal supremacy will receive more extended treatment in a later chapter. But here we may note that in virtue of its primacy the Holy See had the power to intervene in any problems arising out of episcopal elections and especially when unanimity was not achieved and more than one candidate was presented. There were also occasions when bishops succeeded in acquiring from Rome a guarantee of free election for their respective sees. Thus the pope might seem to have been the power which could protect the liberty of the church from lay intrusion. Such, however, was not the case in the ninth and tenth centuries. Occasional popes, such as Nicholas I (858–867),[5] stoutly defended papal prerogatives against rulers and against the overweening ambitions of metropolitans. But too many Roman pontiffs were themselves the victims of the particularly turbulent variety of lay interference practiced by princely factions in the environs of the Eternal City. From this degradation the papacy was rescued by the Saxon kings of Germany who, after the papal coronation of Otto I in 962,

---

[5] With popes, as with kings and emperors, the dates given after the ruler's name refer to his pontificate or reign, not to his entire life.

were also rulers of Rome and north Italy. Otto I (936–973) maintained that no pope should be elected without his consent. His successors, beginning with Otto III (983–1002), often appointed popes. The result was a vast improvement in the morale of the Holy See. German emperors were loyal Christians who took seriously their responsibility in church and government. Henry II (1002–1024) was canonized as a saint. But manifestly there was no recovery of ecclesiastical liberty. German Holy Roman Emperors were simply extending to Italy what they had been practicing north of the Alps.

Lay interference in ecclesiastical matters was only partly the consequence of the secular aspects of a bishop's position. Contemporary theory and practice tended to merge, even to confuse, temporal and spiritual authority. Not only was the bishop's status partly political; the king was commonly regarded as a quasi-ecclesiastical functionary. Indeed, so close was the association of things lay and things religious and so deeply rooted was the tradition that kingly authority had a religious aspect that many rulers held the bishopric to be in their gift. This privilege was often signified by a ceremony known as lay investiture. Before a bishop entered upon his jurisdiction, he was solemnly invested by the king with the symbols of his office, the ring and the episcopal staff or crozier. Actually, this meant that a layman conferred the ecclesiastical power of jurisdiction.

Until the middle years of the eleventh century, lay investiture occasioned no particular opposition. The king's quasi-priestly functions were generally accepted. In point of fact, power was exercised for the most part loyally and with a genuine regard for the welfare of the church. Nevertheless, lay investiture was a striking example of the extent to which the church had fallen under lay control. Abuse of this privilege could be dangerous indeed. Thus it was that the opponents of lay control seized upon lay investiture as the heart of the matter and directed their energies toward its abolition. In the second half of the eleventh century, a reform movement gained sufficient momentum to challenge ancient and long-accepted practices. Since the impetus for this enterprise was provided by a monastic organization, it will be well first to consider the state of monasticism during the feudal age.

Monasticism in the Feudal Age

Monasticism, the corporate and regulated asceticism of religious devoting their lives to prayer and worship, is very old. In Christian history it had early made its appearance in the Near East, especially in the desert regions around Alexandria. Strictly speaking, most of these desert "monks" were hermits living a solitary life. In 379 St. Basil organized a regulated monastic establishment which proved to be a model for others. Later the Emperor Justinian (527–565) officially authorized the universal adoption of the rules then ascribed to Basil.

Various monastic ventures soon made their appearance in western Europe, a particularly significant example being in Ireland. Indeed, by the sixth century Irish Christianity was predominantly monastic and abbots enjoyed greater authority than bishops. Irish monasticism was also extremely austere, as is evidenced by the Rule of St. Columbanus (b. 543, d. 615). Among other things, great emphasis was laid on distant journeying as penance, a sort of exile from home for Christ. As a consequence Irish monks became famous as missionaries, and it was they who evangelized

Scotland and northern England. In fact, the name Scotland results from the immigration of these monks and others from Ireland, the contemporary term for Irishmen being *Scoti.*

It should be observed also that Irish and Anglo-Saxon Christianity managed to preserve a lively tradition of Biblical and classical scholarship. Partly because their native speech was not confounded with a vulgarized spoken Latin, they painstakingly studied the ancient manuals of grammar and became accomplished Latinists. In addition, Celtic and Anglo-Saxon manuscripts of the Dark Ages are among the most handsome now in existence.

Although St. Columbanus and other *Scoti* had penetrated the continent, it was the Rule drawn up by St. Benedict of Nursia in 529 which was to be adopted universally in the West. These regulations, which, as many have observed, temper asceticism with a "Roman" sense of order and moderation, were supplemented with a view to greater uniformity by a code published at the Council of Aachen in 817. The Emperor Louis the Pious, Charlemagne's successor, who had authorized these measures, had been advised by St. Benedict of Aniane.

The primary purpose of the monastic life, it must be remembered, was orderly corporate prayer. Monks, preeminently among mediaeval Christians, dedicated their lives to rendering suitable homage to God. They vowed to renounce all personal possessions (poverty), to forego marriage (chastity), and to obey their superior, the abbot, in all things (obedience). Further, they were to remain attached to one monastery (stability) and not wander from abbey to abbey. A year's novitiate or trial preceded the taking of these final vows.

The Rule itself centers around the *Opus Dei*, the recitation of the canonical offices or services—matins, lauds, vespers, and so on—at the appointed hours. Everything else is secondary, and the notable achievements of monks in learning, agriculture, and the like were, to use a familiar modern expression, extracurricular. Indeed, asceticism was not deemed good in itself, but only insofar as it contributed to the fundamental monastic purpose: prayer, worship, and the sanctification of the soul.

St. Benedict was a practical person with a keen knowledge of human nature. Excessive ascetism was as much to be avoided as laxity, but "idleness is the enemy of the soul." The Rule provides for a healthy change of activity, in short for recreation. "The brethren ought to be occupied at specified times in manual labor, and at other fixed hours in holy reading." Farm labor was not specifically enjoined unless necessary. "If, however, the nature of the place or poverty require their labor at gathering in the harvest, let them not grieve at that, for then are they truly monks when they live by the labor of their hands as our Fathers and the Apostles did. Let everything, however, be done with moderation for the sake of the faint-hearted." [6]

In the course of time the monastic agricultural estate came to be a familiar feature of the mediaeval countryside. In fact, such establishments as a consequence of their regular routine, their experience, and the added knowledge gained by experimentation in agricultural techniques undoubtedly contributed much to mediaeval agrarian progress.

Similarly, monastic study and reading made its contribution to mediaeval learning. Cassiodorus, a minister of state

[6] Quotations from *The Rule of St. Benedict*, tr. by Cardinal Gasquet (The Medieval Library, ed. Sir Israel Gollancz; London, 1925), pp. 84–85.

under the Ostrogothic king Theodoric (d. 526) and a contemporary of St. Benedict, founded a monastery which he
endowed with his own library and in which he arranged that
the monks copy manuscripts as well as study them. The
practice spread, and to the monastic writing rooms (*scrip-
toria*) we owe the preservation not only of important religious works, but also of the pagan classics. In addition, some
abbeys kept records of local happenings, and these monastic
chronicles are among the significant historical sources for
early mediaeval history.

Although monks were normally dedicated to a life of
prayer, they were sometimes sent out of the monastery as
missionaries. A celebrated example is St. Augustine, who in
597 was sent by Pope Gregory the Great to Anglo-Saxon
Britain. The Christianity which he established there and
which was centered at Canterbury grew slowly and with
difficulty. By the mid-seventh century, however, it had
begun to absorb the Celtic church of the north. Celtic Christians were reluctant to abandon certain ecclesiastical usages
which differed from the Roman, but the latter officially
triumphed at the Synod of Whitby (664). Eventually the
entire British Isles conformed.

The Benedictine Rule, therefore, spread throughout all
western Europe, gradually replacing other systems. It was
also adopted by women, and although the precise relation
of the early nunneries to the Benedictine system is obscure,
it is known that Charlemagne propagated a form of the Rule
for the nunneries of his empire. Clearly monasticism in both
its religious and nonreligious aspects was an important feature of mediaeval life. It produced a new type of clergy,
known as the "regular" because its members lived according
to a rule (*regula*). They were distinguished from the ordi-

nary priests and bishops who lived in the world and came to be known as the secular clergy (from *saeculum*, time). Some idea of the significance of monasticism can be obtained from the fact that by 1300 there were some 37,000 Benedictine monks in western Europe. This figure does not include the many men and women of other orders which were founded during the Middle Ages. Moreover, of those monks who for one reason or another were drawn out of the normal cloistered life, many became bishops, cardinals, and even popes.

The effects of feudal conditions on the secular clergy, the priests and the bishops, have already been observed. Since the monastic life requires peace and security and since these were rarely to be had in the feudal age, monasticism faced a serious crisis in the early tenth century. For one thing, monastic establishments, especially those which were well endowed, suffered heavily during the Norse invasions, far more heavily, in fact, than other religious foundations which were better protected. As in the case of the bishopric, the abbey too became feudalized. In many instances, its church and its lands and all its possessions, a complex of properties and jurisdictions both religious and secular called the *abbatia*, were incorporated into the domain of a seigneur. Often this was justified by the original foundation. The seigneur, king, bishop, or noble, or his successors, retained jurisdiction over what was originally endowed. Then, in the period when the Carolingian empire was divided and subdivided, subsequent alienations placed monasteries in the hands of magnates of varied rank and importance.

According to the Benedictine Rule and even older regulations of canon law, an abbot, the head of a monastery, was chosen by the monks, not necessarily by a majority vote, but rather by the *maior et sanior pars,* that is, a corporate decision based on the quality as well as the number of participants. Votes, in other words, were weighed not counted. Disputed elections were judged by the bishop, who, even if the choice were unanimous, could for cause refuse to institute the nominee. Actually, of course, this ideal rule was widely flouted, and the abbot was frequently appointed by the local feudal proprietor. Choice made in this manner was not necessarily bad. There were many royal or ducal abbeys throughout the various divisions of the former Carolingian empire whose heads were men of religious quality. But the temptation to appoint men of secular interests was great, especially in a warlike age. After all, military defense was a real necessity. Nobles who found it difficult to maintain the requisite number of knights inevitably turned to the monastic properties in their domains for additional military aid. As a consequence men entirely strangers to the communities they managed, sometimes even laymen, were installed as abbots. Such persons could fulfill all the secular functions of the *abbatia*, including military service, and leave the actual monastic responsibilities to a subordinate. Hugh Capet (987–996), founder of the French dynasty which bore his name, was abbot of several houses.[7] This procedure, furthermore, was not clearly prohibited by canon law. True, the Benedictine Rule stipulated that the abbot should be a monk, but no special blessing, certainly nothing comparable to episcopal consecration, was deemed indispensable. The more scrupulous proprietors took minor orders, which entailed no serious religious obligations, but even this practice was not consistently followed.

Toward the second half of the eleventh century, when reform was already in progress, a way out of this anomalous

[7] The nickname *Capet*, or *Chapet*, signifies "ecclesiastical cloak."

situation was discovered. While maintaining full mastery over the *abbatia*, the magnate would designate some properly qualified monk as abbot. In some cases the monks were even allowed to elect their abbot although the lord usually retained the right of solemnly investing their nominee. A number of lay abbacies were thus relinquished to religious rule, and again Hugh Capet serves as a good example, for he gave up several of his monasteries.

The reason for this lay intrusion was, as in the case of the bishop or priest, political and economic. Most laymen had no interest in religious authority as such. They wanted to control persons within their domains, and they needed the material resources of the ecclesiastical establishments. It must be admitted that contemporary conditions very largely justified these demands. It was only the abuse of power which could and did cause the grave scandals that provoked the wave of reforms.

An abbot, however chosen, was expected to take an oath of fealty and to perform the usual feudal obligations, court service, the provision of soldiers for his lord's army, and financial aid. The feudal obligations of hospitality fell especially heavily on monasteries. This should not be confused with the injunction in the Benedictine Rule to treat all strangers as though they were Christ himself. Rather it was a feudal burden. It was not uncommon for a seigneur to descend on a monastery with a large retinue including horses and dogs for the chase. On such occasions, the abbey would require the tenants of its estates to make the necessary contributions. Not infrequently the result was ruinous, and there are cases in which monasteries were forced to dissolve after such visitations.

Fortunately, wholesale pillage of monastic assets sometimes weighed on the conscience of even the more hardened seigneurs. At any rate, a certain number felt called upon to recompense the abbeys in their jurisdiction by reserving to the monks a specified portion of their revenues.

Far more serious than the appropriation of monastic goods was the consequent decline in morale and discipline. If there were reasonably conscientious lay abbots, there were also those who installed themselves and their families, even their horses and dogs, right in the monastery. Soon the monks imitated the worldly life of the "abbot." If discipline broke down completely, as occasionally it did, monks married, lived with their families, and gave up all pretense of religious life.

It was scandals such as these which disturbed the reformers. Lay control could be tolerated so long as laymen conscientiously respected the ecclesiastical responsibilities which they assumed. This had been the case, for example, under Charlemagne. But as abuses multiplied, it was felt that lay interference was at the root of most of the church's troubles. Accordingly the reformers directed their efforts against all lay interference. Before the mediaeval reformation is considered, however, it will be well to treat further some of the achievements of monks outside the cloister.

In two nonreligious fields of human endeavor Benedictine monks made important contributions. These were agriculture and learning. There was a systematic regularity about the management of monastic estates which insured efficient operation. Monks usually possessed the Roman books on agriculture, and they often pioneered with new experiments. It is now known that agricultural techniques improved in the Dark Ages, and presumably much of the improvement resulted from monastic enterprise.

The library was an essential part of any well-equipped monastery. Some were small, possessing only a minimum of scriptural and liturgical works. But since the copying of manuscripts was encouraged as a form of activity, monastic libraries expanded. Valued first as examples of Latin style, they were subsequently prized for their literary worth. Thus there could develop in the Middle Ages a genuine appreciation of ancient literature.

CHAPTER II

The Church
and the Reform of Society

Early Efforts: The Cluny Reform Movement

THAT the evils in the church reflected the barbarous character of the feudal age is evident in what has already been described. It would be incorrect, however, to assume that the church entirely abdicated its spiritual position. Individual and collective efforts, though not as numerous or as effective as were needed, were directed at the worst misconduct of lay officials.

Against heavy odds and, it must be admitted, without too much success, the church also struggled to maintain the peace. Depredations were numerous. Innocent people suffered, and church property was often pillaged. Toward the end of the tenth century certain local synods in southern France proclaimed the "Peace of God," which placed under severe ecclesiastical censure all who attacked clergy or church property. Later the poor and even merchants were included. The Peace of God was not altogether successful, since few lay authorities gave it adequate support. A little later, and somewhat more effective because it did receive some backing from the laity, was the "Truce of God," which attempted to prohibit private warfare on certain days and during certain seasons.

Although efforts such as these were local and in the long run unavailing, they show that many ecclesiastics and lay-men were aware of the problems which beset feudal society and were determined to combat them. As their numbers in-creased, so did their courage. Eventually, out of experience came effective organization. By the eleventh century, re-form was indeed in progress, and there began a veritable transformation of western European society. It commenced with a reform of monasticism, and the spirit and method by which it advanced stemmed largely, though not entirely, from Cluny, the monastery founded by Duke William of Aquitaine in 910.

The Cluny movement—for so it has been called—stood for two things above all: the restoration of monastic disci-pline and the liberation of monasticism from lay control. In pursuing the first objective, the early abbots of Cluny, of whom St. Odo (926–942) and St. Odilo (994–1049) were among the most celebrated, actually effected some impor-tant alterations in the Benedictine system. In order to achieve the ideal of perpetual collective prayer, the offices—that is, the services which the monks chanted together—were multiplied and lengthened. In fact, Cluny contributed significantly to the artistic elaboration of the church's lit-urgy. Music, the chant, was developed, and the great Ro-manesque abbey church stood as testimony of the con-temporary association between art and religion. Cluny also emphasized the service to the poor.

All this left less time for other monastic activities, and some have held that the healthy balance between prayer and other useful occupations which had characterized the Benedictine Rule was upset. The Benedictine tradition of study, especially of the classics, languished. And perhaps because a larger proportion of monks were ordained priests, manual labor was not encouraged.

Another innovation was the association of more than one house with a single center. Some of the Cluny abbots traveled widely and successfully spread the idea of monastic regeneration. Sometimes other abbeys requested Cluny to assume a kind of suzerainty over them. Others took in monastic "colonists" sent from Cluny. Thus, in one way or another, Cluny became the head of a great movement which spread throughout Europe. By the twelfth century the abbot of Cluny was recognized as the titular head of over three hundred houses. This was a distinct break with the Benedictine system of autonomous abbeys.

There was also a tendency for monasteries to place their foundations under the immediate protection of the Holy See. In return for a payment, or *census* as it was called, rarely more than nominal, the pope might concede emancipation from the jurisdiction of the local bishop. The importance of this procedure lay in its emphasis on the central authority of Rome and the consequent curtailment of episcopal power. Monasteries so freed were no longer subject to the bishop's visitation, and his presence was required only for such occasions as the conferring of the sacrament of holy orders on monastic candidates for the priesthood. The results were not always happy, and there were a number of misunderstandings between bishops and abbots, misunderstandings which were to be a source of conflict and even scandal until the jurisdictional ambiguity was resolved by the Council of

Trent in the sixteenth century. Notwithstanding, the practice continued. Eventually all Cluny houses and many others came under the immediate jurisdiction of the Holy See.

The second feature of the Cluny reform program, the liberation of monasteries from lay control, presented a different sort of problem and led finally to some acrimonious disputes with prominent laymen. But it was not always so. The fact that Cluny itself had been guaranteed freedom in its foundation charter is an indication that some laymen were beginning to realize that times were changing. During the turbulent days of invasion and feudal disorder, there had been considerable justification for procedures which provided physical security for the monasteries. The need for such protection was, however, passing; and some lay seigneurs, prompted by the same sort of piety which had induced their predecessors to endow abbeys, now often guaranteed emancipation. A sizable number of seigneurs also abandoned the *abbatia*, the control of the abbey estate and revenue. In a sense this was a restitution by one lord of property and jurisdiction appropriated by a predecessor. Although some sort of supervision was frequently retained, the emphasis was on protection, not control, by an "advocate," as the lord was often called.

Reform Spreads to the Entire Church: The Age of Hildebrand

Important as was Cluny, it was not the only center of reform. Lorraine, for example, was also an area of significant activity. Moreover, although the primary purpose of the Cluny movement was the rehabilitation of monasticism, an impetus was provided for an equally important regeneration of the secular clergy. By the middle of the eleventh century,

Rome's leadership in the entire endeavor was evident. It should also be added that some of the rulers of Europe lent their willing co-operation even though it was apparent that whatever ecclesiastical jurisdiction they enjoyed was now challenged. A striking example is the Holy Roman Emperor Henry III (1039–1056), whose papal appointee, Leo IX (1049–1054), contributed materially to the strengthening of Rome's leadership.

Pope Leo IX, formerly Bruno of Toul and a Lorrainer, threw all his energies into combating prevailing abuses. He traveled wherever he could and summoned local clergy to reforming councils. To places he could not himself visit, he sent his legates. Accordingly, after Leo's pontificate there was no doubt that Rome was assuming its proper role as head of the church.

In the year 1059 there was enacted at Rome a decree providing for the election of the pope. The Roman bishop, it was stated, was thenceforth to be chosen by seven (later six) cardinal bishops, those who occupied the principal sees in the environs of the city. A somewhat larger number of cardinal priests, pastors of certain prominent Roman parishes, and cardinal deacons approved the choice. The people acclaimed the nominee. Thus the ancient canonical principle of election by clergy and people was preserved in form while the actual election by local clerics was guaranteed.

Leo IX and his immediate successors were ably assisted by a former monk, Hildebrand, who occupied the important position of archdeacon. Hildebrand was destined, as Pope Gregory VII (1073–1085), to leave a lasting impression on his time, and to many historians this is the "age of Hildebrand" or the "Gregorian era." Because Gregory's energetic measures resulted in a bitter struggle with the Holy

Roman Emperor Henry IV, his career has been variously estimated. To some he has seemed too intransigent, too eager to exalt papal authority. It is true that he had compiled a set of propositions, the *Dictatus papae*, which clearly stated Rome's supremacy. That the political implications of some of these propositions as well as certain of his actions were probably not fully understood by Gregory will be explained later. But it should be emphasized here that Gregory was neither a lawyer nor a politician. He was a mystic, a profoundly holy man who felt the divine presence in his soul. Whatever ambition he had was not for himself. Nor did he seek power for its own sake. In short, he was a monk whose heart ardently burned with a zeal to Christianize society.

Gregory began by reinforcing the policies of his predecessors. His legates traveled everywhere, and decrees against simony, clerical marriage, and such abuses multiplied. He met opposition in many places, and the prohibition of clerical marriage caused considerable individual hardship. But Gregory was generally supported by popular opinion and in the long run won out. As a consequence clerical morale was distinctly raised.

In one matter this energetic pope went a step beyond his predecessors. The famous decree of 1075 prohibiting lay investiture challenged the rulers of Europe. The subsequent investiture controversy, as it is often called, was a logical culmination of the church's struggle against secular encroachment. It was not equally severe in every country. The king of France, Philip I, for example, attempted some resistance, but his temperament and his extreme obesity rendered him unfit for any sustained action. Gregory evidently thought it unwise to press William the Conqueror of England, who at least appointed worthy bishops. Somewhat later

(1107), St. Anselm, a distinguished archbishop of Canterbury, after prolonged conflict with William II and Henry I was able to arrange a compromise on the matter of investiture.

The most spectacular controversy occurred in the Holy Roman Empire. This was so for two reasons. First, in the empire more than in any other part of Christendom, bishops tended to be counts and, therefore, directly associated with government. Second, the young Emperor Henry IV was stubbornly insistent on maintaining a control over ecclesiastics precisely because they were governmental officials. The young emperor summoned a council of German bishops who, as royal appointees, were for the most part loyal and agreed to the deposition of Gregory. Henry then wrote a letter to the pope which closes in the following violent language:

Thou, therefore, damned by this curse and by the judgment of all our bishops and ourselves, come down and relinquish the apostolic chair which thou has usurped. Let another assume the seat of St. Peter, who will not practice violence under the cloak of religion, but will teach St. Peter's wholesome doctrine. I, Henry, king by the grace of God, together with all our bishops, say unto thee: "Come down, come down, to be damned throughout all eternity!"

At a synod held in Rome somewhat later in 1075, various bishops who had subscribed to the action in Germany were excommunicated. Following is the sentence pronounced against Siegfried, archbishop of Mainz:

In accordance with the judgment of the Holy Spirit and by the authority of the blessed Apostles Peter and Paul, we suspend from every episcopal function, and exclude from the com-

munion of the body and blood of the Lord, Siegfried, archbishop of Mainz, who has attempted to cut off the bishops and
abbots of Germany from the Holy Roman Church, their spiritual mother—unless perchance in the hour of death, and then
only if he shall come to himself and truly repent.

Gregory then solemnly anathematized Henry "since he
has refused to obey as a Christian should or to return to the
God whom he has abandoned by taking part with excommunicated persons . . . and has separated himself from thy
Church." [1]

Excommunication is the most severe penalty the church
can inflict. It deprives the one excommunicated of all sacraments until he is willing to repent and make whatever restitution is necessary. Since it is presumed that because of his
offense he is in a state of mortal sin, his immortal soul is
gravely endangered. There are also political implications in
the excommunication of a ruler, for his subjects associate
with him at their peril. Indeed, Gregory in his sentence
against Henry specifically deposed the emperor and ab-
solved his subjects from their oath of allegiance.

Whether Gregory fully realized the political consequences of his action is debatable. But the fact remains that
Henry was faced with a serious situation. Indeed, many of
his lay vassals regarded the excommunication as a heaven-
sent sanction for rebellion. It was to force the pope's hand,
therefore, that the young ruler crossed the Alps in winter.
At Canossa, where Gregory was staying, he stood in the
snow as a penitent. The pope hesitated. Since the emperor
was willing to make the necessary promises, however, he

[1] Quotations from *The Correspondence of Pope Gregory VII*. tr.
by Ephraim Emerton, Columbia University Records of Civilization,
Vol. XIV (New York: Columbia University Press, 1932), pp. 90–91.

as a priest was bound to absolve the contrite sinner. As a result Henry was reinstated.

Despite later interpretations representing Canossa as the humiliation of state before church, it was Henry, not Gregory, who now had the advantage. He soon resumed his former practices and, as Gregory delayed action, gained strength sufficient to defy a second excommunication and deposition. When the pope died in southern Italy, a virtual prisoner of the Normans who had "rescued" him, Henry's troops were in command of Rome.

It is a tribute, however, to Gregory's devotion and to the solid achievements of his predecessors that in the long run his cause triumphed. Worthy successors carried the work forward. Urban II (1088–1099), the pope who launched the First Crusade, was particularly successful. Equally firm in principle, he was more diplomatic and moderate in practice. At length a settlement was reached at Worms in 1122. This concordat, or agreement, which followed closely that earlier arranged in England, formally abolished lay investiture of the ring and crozier, the symbols of the bishop's spiritual jurisdiction. The emperor might present the scepter, symbol of temporal power, and he was permitted to be present at the election. Thus, although lay investiture was ended, lay interference in elections was not entirely obviated.

The Early Twelfth Century: St. Bernard of Clairvaux

It has been frequently observed of western monasticism that it possesses a remarkable capacity for self-renewal and an ability to adapt itself to changing circumstances. Hence its variety. Cluny answered admirably a great need for re-

form and for an organization which could combat the de-
centralizing tendencies of feudalism. Its abbots exercised
considerable ecclesiastical influence, and among their number were men of great distinction. Peter the Venerable
(1122–1157), for example, scholar as well as churchman,
was one of the finest characters of the twelfth century. By
the early twelfth century, however, many Cluny houses had
become richly endowed establishments with handsome
abbey churches and costly furnishings. In certain instances,
discipline suffered. This did not mean that there were such
pronounced scandals as in the turbulent days of early feudalism. Yet the departure from Benedictine simplicity elicited
criticism. Thus it was that the Cluny reform was followed
by others.

In Italy, St. Romuald (d. 1027) provided a combination
of the eremitical and the corporate monastic life later known
as the Camaldolese order. In 1084, a German, St. Bruno,
founded a community, at La Grande Chartreuse in the
French Alps, in which monks maintained almost complete
silence and abstained totally from meat. Here was an exclusive dedication to prayer and worship. Although the
order was not officially approved until late in the twelfth
century, constitutions were drawn up in 1128. Perhaps best
known for a liqueur invented in the nineteenth century, the
Carthusians may boast that they are one of the very few
orders which have continued to the present day without
need of reform.

It remained, however, for the Cistercians to accomplish
for the twelfth century what the Cluniacs had done for the
eleventh. That they did so was largely owing to the efforts
of St. Bernard of Clairvaux (b. 1090, d. 1153). It was in 1113
that Bernard, then a young nobleman, brought with him to

the Benedictine abbey at Cîteaux a band of companions in-
tent upon an austere monastic life. Cîteaux had been founded
by St. Robert of Molesmes and was dedicated to a literal
observance of the Benedictine Rule. It had faced many dis-
couragements. Now it received a new lease on life. In 1115,
Bernard was sent to found a new house at Clairvaux which,
in fact, proved to be the first of 163 abbeys established by
this energetic monk.

The order—for a separate and distinct monastic organization came into being—was given constitutions drawn up
by an Englishman, Stephen Harding, and, in 1119, approved
by the pope. The Cistercians wore a white habit which distinguished them from the Benedictine black. The regime of
fast and abstinence was severe, and no elaborate furnishings
were permitted in Cistercian abbey churches. Hence in a
period which saw the flowering of mediaeval art, Cistercian
abbeys were plain and unadorned, though often of exquisite
design. As an organization the Cistercian order avoided at
once Cluniac centralization and Benedictine isolation. Each
monastery was self-governing under its abbot, but periodical
general chapters of abbots preserved uniformity. By 1152
there were some 350 abbeys.

Like Cluny earlier, the Cistercian order was also associated
with contemporary social developments. The white monks
preferred remote and solitary places and were often found
in the frontier regions of mediaeval Europe. The German
expansion eastward owed much to them. They were also
active in some of the newly discovered mining regions.
In the Low Countries they pioneered in reclaiming land
from the sea, and in England they were prominent in the
production of wool. But these were the nonreligious achievements of the Cistercians and were in considerable part the

work of lay brothers, *conversi*, as they were called. The Cistercian Rule, however, placed great emphasis on manual labor for the monks themselves and, although exceptions were made in frontier regions, forbade the employment of peasants.

Not only the Cistercian order but the church as a whole owed an immense debt to St. Bernard. Even a cursory account of this extraordinary man's career would fill a chapter. He was constantly journeying—usually against his inclinations—across Europe as the adviser of popes and kings. He preached the Second Crusade and formulated the rule for the religio-military order of Knights Templar. He eloquently opposed innovation in doctrine and withstood the redoubtable Abelard. He composed many sermons and hymns, some of which are still familiar. When one of his own brethren became pope as Eugenius III, he prepared for him a famous treatise, entitled *De consideratione*, of which the theme is the necessity of meditation before action. St. Bernard had no sympathy with the busy and somewhat worldly papal *curia*.

It might well be asked how he found time for the ideal of his own heart, the religious life. Indeed, he repeatedly complained that he was drawn away from it. Yet, since he possessed to an unusual degree the capacity to withdraw from temporal distractions, even when surrounded by them, he lived in contemplation of things spiritual. To this transcendent capacity Dante paid tribute, when in his celebrated poem, the *Divine Comedy*, he placed St. Bernard close to the divine presence in paradise. With equal justice, historians have often called the first half of the twelfth century the "age of St. Bernard."

A contemporary of St. Bernard, St. Norbert (b. 1080,

d. 1134), founded the canons regular of Prémontré (near Laon in France) or Premonstratensian canons. The Rule, drawn up by Norbert's followers, was based mainly on the Rule of St. Augustine, but was influenced by other systems. At least some education was required of candidates, and progress in knowledge was a prerequisite to ordination to the priesthood. The Rule, moreover, emphasized the service which Premonstratensian canons were to render the parish churches in their neighborhoods. In short, Premonstratensian houses were centers of missionary activity dedicated to raising the morale of local clergy.

Thus by the middle years of the twelfth century the church had been transformed from an institution struggling to preserve its integrity against the centrifugal forces of an imperfectly civilized feudal society into an organization of authority capable of exerting an influence of its own. Clerical morale had been measurably raised. A marked increase in the number and quality of schools was beginning to have a salutary effect on the training of the clergy. Lay society, too, had changed. The days of turbulence and chronic insecurity were over. A spacious period of positive achievement was opening, and to the story of the church in this happier age we now turn.

CHAPTER III

The Church
in the High Middle Ages

THE twelfth and thirteenth centuries are sometimes designated the "high Middle Ages" because in that period what
we have come to regard as mediaeval civilization reached
a climax. It was a time of diminishing feudalism and more
competent government, of commerce and towns, of money
and credit, of increasing and freer agriculture, of learning
and art.[1] The area affected by western European civilization in 1300 was considerably larger than in the year 1000.
Mediaeval feudal society was dynamic, and thousands of
knights, merchants, peasants, and missionaries pushed the
frontiers outward or passed overseas to found settlements
in the Levant. The problems this expanding mediaeval civilization presented to the church were many and varied, but
the church was better equipped to meet them. Much as contemporary kingdoms perfected new systems of administration, so the church improved its instrument of government.
This structure has been called, not inaptly, the papal monarchy.

[1] See Sidney Painter, *The Rise of the Feudal Monarchies* and
Mediaeval Society (both Ithaca, N.Y., 1951).

Ecclesiastical Government: The Papal Monarchy

The mediaeval papal monarchy is the elaboration in government of the primitive doctrine that the bishop of Rome, the successor of St. Peter, chief of the apostles, was supreme in the church. Since early feudal conditions had made the exercise of papal supremacy difficult and sometimes almost impossible, the restoration of this supremacy was, as has been remarked, an important objective of the eleventh-century reformers. There is an additional factor. The mediaeval revival of government, both ecclesiastical and secular, owed much to the concurrent study of law. The university of Bologna, which emerged during the later years of the twelfth century, was noted for its teaching of Roman civil law. Together with other institutions in different parts of Europe, it also emphasized church law, or canon law as it is called.

This canon law was to the constitution of the church what civil law was to secular government. It defined the rights, duties, and powers of all ecclesiastical persons, of all ecclesiastical institutions, and of laymen in their relations with these. It was, therefore, the law administered in all ecclesiastical courts from those of the bishops up to that of the pope. Further, the jurisdiction of canon law was wider in the Middle Ages than has been the case in more recent times. All cases involving ecclesiastical persons—and this would include men in minor orders and students at ecclesiastical institutions, in short all "clerks"—and all cases of a religious nature or cases involving sacraments, oaths, usury, and the like were heard in ecclesiastical courts.

Canon law was primarily based on the Bible, the writings of the early church fathers, and the decrees of councils and

popes. What happened in the eleventh and twelfth centuries
was the systematizing of the church's law. Sometime between 1139 and 1141, for example, Gratian published a
treatise or code of canon law, the *Concordantia discordan-
tium canonum* or *Harmony of Discordant Canons*. Moreover, the process commenced here was developed further
in the thirteenth century as certain popes added and authorized new collections or decretals. All these emphasized
the role of the papacy as the fountainhead of ecclesiastical
law.

It is not altogether surprising, therefore, that whereas
most of the popes in the century or more preceding 1150
were monks and associated with a reform which in its origins
was monastic, those after 1150 were mainly canon lawyers.
Their contribution to the church's constitution reflects their
legal training. Moreover, since certain of these distinguished
pontiffs are best known for their controversies with kings
and emperors, their efforts in behalf of ecclesiastical government are often overlooked. Alexander III (1159–1181), for
example, with the help of the Lombard cities successfully
opposed the Emperor Frederick Barbarossa (1152–1190).
He also summoned the important Third Lateran Council of
1179. Similarly, Innocent III (1198–1216) tends to be
known more for his dealing with several contemporary rulers than for his achievements in ecclesiastical affairs. His
accomplishments in this latter field, however, were of the
greatest importance, particularly in his efforts to reform the
church, to combat heresy, and to promote the crusade. The
Fourth Lateran Council of 1215, to which further reference
will presently be made, was undoubtedly his most significant
achievement. Gregory IX (1227–1241) and Innocent IV
(1243–1254), the principal opponents of the Holy Roman

Emperor Frederick II, were also great churchmen. Gregory IX issued a collection of decretals which further amplified the body of canon law. Innocent IV sent out the first missionary-ambassadors to the Mongols and thus inaugurated an important contact between Europe and the Far East which endured for about a century.

Because Innocent III was perhaps the most distinguished of all the mediaeval popes, it has become almost a tradition to single out his pontificate for a study of mediaeval ecclesiastical government at its best. On the whole, the tradition is justified; and in the following pages this great pontiff's name will appear frequently. A certain caution, however, is required in thus emphasizing Innocent III's achievements. First, he was hardly a typical pope. A young man—he was only thirty-seven on his accession—he was educated at Paris and Bologna and was a skilled theologian as well as canonist. Second, owing doubtless to his prominence, he remains a somewhat controversial figure. At first glance his career seems in marked contrast to that of Gregory VII. A determination to promote ecclesiastical reform led Gregory into the realm of political action. Innocent, the lawyer, on the other hand, seems more at home in the political arena. In truth he was, for his training and his special abilities made him so. But this aspect of Innocent's character should not obscure his priestly qualities or the fact that he subscribed to the same fundamental purposes which had motivated Gregory. There is ample evidence, in his voluminous correspondence and in such treatises as *De contemptu mundi*, of a genuine religious spirit. Things spiritual, the supernatural life, came first. Like Gregory, Innocent was a reformer with a high ideal of what the church should be. Close to his heart, too, was the crusade, the recovery of the Holy Places in

Palestine which Gregory had also dreamed of winning.

By the time of Innocent, canon lawyers described the church as a "perfect society," by which they meant that it possessed all the necessary attributes of government. In the exercise of ecclesiastical authority, canon lawyers also distinguished between the power of order and the power of jurisdiction. The former had to do with the sacraments, and in this respect the pope differed in no way from any other bishop. The latter, the power of jurisdiction, embodied government, and to the pope as head of the church was entrusted the "fullness of power." To use modern terminology, he wielded supreme executive, legislative, and judicial authority within the sphere of ecclesiastical government.

To assist him in governing the church, the pope had a *curia* or court much as any mediaeval king had his *curia regis*. The papal *curia* was composed of the cardinals. These, it will be remembered, were the cardinal or principal bishops, priests, and deacons of the city of Rome who in 1059 were designated a body to elect the pope. They were appointed by the pope and in the thirteenth century might number fifty-two if the roster was full. Actually, an average of under thirty seems to have been usual. In 1179 the cardinals were officially organized into a legal corporation, called a "college," with specified duties and perquisites. At the same time the cardinal priests and deacons were permitted actively to participate in papal elections, not merely to approve the choice of the cardinal bishops as had been the case since 1059. Cardinals might be, and indeed often were, of non-Italian origin, but they all resided at Rome. Not until the later Middle Ages did the familiar modern practice originate whereby a cardinal may reside permanently abroad. They were, therefore, clergy of the city of Rome, and their principal function as cardinals was government. In the performance of their duties the cardinals were assisted by a number of secretaries, clerks, notaries, auditors, and the like.

A meeting of the pope with all the cardinals was called a consistory. Innocent III held consistories two or three times a week. But Innocent, it must be remembered, was a comparatively young man of immense energy who felt it his duty to hear personally as many cases as was humanly possible. In later decades, full consistories were reserved for special occasions, and the routine administrative business was relegated to separate bureaus or tribunals. This departmentalization of the papal *curia* was in line with similar measures taken by contemporary secular governments. In each case it represented an advance in the technique of administration.

Not all the curial departments which eventually developed were distinct in the thirteenth century, but those which were will serve as examples of this important governmental process. First in importance was the papal chancery where correspondence was handled. Since the papacy, unlike most secular administrations, had jurisdiction over a tremendous area, the amount of business conducted by letter was enormous. A glance at the registers of any twelfth- or thirteenth-century pope will reveal the scope of papal administration. Moreover, even a brief perusal of the titles of letters sent and received will disclose that, despite the grave crises which history records, the routine of government continued with amazing attention to detail. Indeed, it is no exaggeration to say that this painstaking consideration of individual cases was as important to successful papal government as the more spectacular struggles with kings and emperors.

The chancery developed many procedures worth noting

here. The most important matters were dealt with in documents called greater bulls, from the Latin *bulla* or seal; others were settled in lesser bulls and ordinary letters. Forgery was not uncommon. Chancery experts could detect false documents. To prevent recurrences, great attention was paid to the form of papal charters, the seal, even the points or dots around the seal, and the characteristic Latin style.

The papal financial bureau, the *camera*, was headed by a cardinal-chamberlain (*camerarius*). A particularly distinguished cardinal-chamberlain, who was destined to become Innocent III's successor as Honorius III (1216–1227), drew up in 1192 a *Liber censuum* which contained a list of revenues due the Holy See from its estates and feudal possessions. Revenue from the papal states provided far from sufficient support for this expanding institution. Equally insufficient were other payments such as Peter's pence, which was paid irregularly from certain countries in northern Europe. Most of the papal income came from taxes levied on bishops and other ecclesiastics and from fees exacted at the *curia*. The system never seemed adequate, a fact which goes far to explain the financial worries of the papacy in the later Middle Ages. It should be added, however, that modern economic historians have generally regarded the papal revenue system as a remarkable instrument for its time and a significant contribution to the development of financial administration.

Broadly speaking, most routine curial activity was judicial. By Innocent's time the amount of legal business handled at Rome was enormous, for as a consequence of centralization, the papal *curia* was at once a court of first instance and a court of appeal. Appeals to Rome from local ecclesiastical courts increased tremendously during the high Middle Ages, so much so, in fact, that Innocent III laid down certain conditions under which appeals were to be permitted. Gradually the volume of business forced specialization within the *curia*, and certain separate curial tribunals or courts made an initial appearance in the thirteenth century. This development, however, was to become more clear later. In the sixteenth century the entire *curia* was reorganized into the Congregations which still function. The foundations were laid in the Middle Ages, and important elements were distinct in the thirteenth century.

The Papal Curia *and the Church at Large*

The success of the papal monarchy as a government depended largely on the relations between the *curia* and the bishops. From the time of Gregory VII popes had repeatedly contested with secular rulers the matter of episcopal elections. The investiture controversy resulted in a partial victory for the church, but lay influence in elections and even direct appointment of prelates continued. Convinced that this situation endangered hierarchical efficiency and impeded ecclesiastical policies, successive popes established various precedents for their own intervention in elections. By means of such precedents the popes established the right to intervene in all cases of translation, deposition, and illegal election. Moreover, Rome habitually confirmed the choice of all archbishops and of many bishops and abbots. The Holy See was also by the end of the thirteenth century making "provision" for, that is, appointing, lesser ecclesiastical benefices in an increasing number of instances.

One of the more common cases calling for papal intervention was the disputed election. Perhaps the most celebrated example was the case of Canterbury under King John (1199–1216). It may be recalled that after the Canterbury electors had made their choice the king, who had given his license to elect, forced a second election.[2] Both nominees appealed to Rome, whereupon Innocent III declared both elections invalid and obtained from those electors present in Rome an assent to his own candidate, Stephen Langton. It was some years, however, before King John capitulated.

Bishops, once elected, were held responsible to the Holy See in various ways; and archbishops were required to receive the pallium, a woolen scarf, the symbol of office, from the pope. All bishops had to make periodic visits to Rome, and all might be obliged to attend a general council. Papal legates, usually cardinals, vested with full powers were frequently sent out by the pope, and judge-delegates were appointed to hear certain causes locally. By the mid-thirteenth century certain categories of cases, notably heresy, were specifically reserved to the pope and hence removed from episcopal courts. There were, too, the many appeals from bishops' courts to the *curia*.

Occasionally, when some great issue demanded, the pope summoned a general council. Most bishops and abbots were expected to attend, and representatives of lay rulers often appeared as well. Thus a general council could be a kind of western European assembly. One of the greatest of these gatherings, the Fourth Lateran Council held under Innocent III in 1215, will serve as an illustration. There were present 412 bishops, 800 abbots and priors, and various lay delegates. Committees had so ably prepared the agenda in advance that it required only three weeks for the delegates to complete their work.

The assembled fathers began with a declaration of faith which was largely prompted by the heresies then prevalent,

[2] Painter, *The Rise of the Feudal Monarchies,* pp. 65–66.

especially Catharism then raging in southern France.[3] There was also a re-emphasis on certain traditional doctrines, and there was the famous provision defining the miracle of the Mass as a "transubstantiation" of the bread and wine into Christ's Body and Blood. The doctrine was of primitive origin, but the use of the term "transubstantiation" reflects the progress of theological studies and the demand for precise terminology. Heresy was considered, and the council adopted provisions for handling this problem that foreshadowed the Inquisition.

Innocent's avowed aim to purify the church and complete the work begun in the eleventh century is well illustrated in a series of reform canons. Moreover, a study of these provisions will reveal the vast number and variety of problems which a mediaeval pope faced, as well as the need for unceasing vigilance in maintaining discipline. It will be possible to mention only a few of the most important here. It is noteworthy, for example, that thenceforth clerics were not to dress in a manner or engage in activities calculated to scandalize their calling. A list of occupations absolutely prohibited included the blessing of ordeals. As a consequence that ancient practice gradually died out. Fees for sacraments and for other similar purposes were also forbidden. Bishops were enjoined to preach regularly and to maintain schools for the education of their clergy. Moreover, if scandals persisted among the diocesan clergy, the bishop was himself to be disciplined. A number of canons dealt with the regular clergy and their relations with the bishops. All orders were to hold periodic meetings of abbots.

One celebrated canon has affected the lives of Roman Catholics to this day. Under pain of excommunication, each

[3] For Catharism, see pp. 63–65.

person must receive the sacraments of penance and the Eucharist at least once a year. Presumably the regulation indicates that many were avoiding this irreducible minimum of observance. Indeed, it is worth noting that, so far as can be determined, reception of the sacraments by the laity was far less frequent in the Middle Ages than had been the custom in the primitive church or than is now the custom in modern times.

Many other canons were enacted, but these may give some idea of how such a council operated and the situations with which it dealt. It should be observed further that there was discussion of current political matters, such as the disposition of the lands of the count of Toulouse, the succession to the imperial throne, and Stephen Langton's support of the English barons against King John, now reconciled to the church. There remains the question whether the reforms were carried out. It is a difficult question to answer and would require detailed study of every diocese in Christendom. Later complaints would seem to indicate that not all bishops shared Innocent III's zeal. Nor were all dioceses able to sustain their efforts. It does appear, however, that despite some weaknesses the level of ecclesiastical morale was considerably higher in 1250 than in 1050. This the church had accomplished in two centuries of perseverance. Councils such as the Fourth Lateran played no small part in this accomplishment.

In concluding this discussion of the relations between the *curia* and the church at large it may be appropriate to add a word about the ecclesiastical penalty known as the interdict. Interdict is a kind of "territorial excommunication." A given area is deprived of most of the sacraments as a disciplinary

measure in extremely grave circumstances. Like excommunication, the interdict was imposed rarely. Since it affected
many people, it was more serious than the excommunication
of a single person. It was used, for example, by Pope Innocent III against both France and England with the purpose
of bringing popular pressure to bear on King Philip Augustus and King John. The former eventually reinstated his
wife, Ingebourg, whom he had formerly repudiated; the latter finally accepted Innocent's candidate for the see of Canterbury, Stephen Langton.

In the case of the interdict placed upon England in 1208,
the clergy were given a number of detailed instructions governing their conduct and their relations with the laity. "The
altars of the churches were to be stripped. . . . Infants were
to be baptized in their homes . . . with all due solemnity,"
but marriages were not to be contracted, and no priest was
to be present at the burial of the dead. He might, however,
"while the body remained at home, without cross or holy
water, privately commend the soul of the departed. . . .
Whoever shall seek confession may have it whenever he
wishes, and legitimate testimony be given, but without eucharist or extreme unction."

Priests were also instructed to assemble people before a
cross set up out of doors "on Sundays and special feasts and
diligently preach patience and obedience, because Christ
was made obedient to the Father. . . . And let the priests
say prayers most devoutly for the peace of the church and
for the lord king that our Lord Jesus Christ may lead his
steps in the way of salvation. . . . Let prayers be said for
the living and for the dead as is customary on bended knees
and let the people be most earnestly urged to pray day and

night so that the absence of masses may be remedied by vigils and supplications." [4]

The Friars

Innocent III was a busy pope, and although a deeply religious man, he was not particularly sympathetic to extremes of devotion or novel practices. Moreover, a canon of the Fourth Lateran Council provided that there should be no additional religious orders. On one occasion he was visited by a poorly clad, barefoot pilgrim who requested authorization for himself and a small band of followers dedicated to the systematic pursuit of apostolic poverty. Innocent, absorbed in the multifarious cares of his office, was at first inclined to refuse categorically. But something in his visitor's manner impressed him. Instead, he told the pilgrim to return the following day.

There is a story, memorialized in a painting by the Italian artist Giotto (d. 1336), which relates that during the night the pope dreamed that the church of St. John Lateran was about to fall and the same barefooted pilgrim came and supported the building with his shoulder. Innocent, in any case, was too discerning not to realize that devoted men leading Christlike lives might shame others into better conduct. Accordingly he gave a verbal sanction to his visitor's request.

The man whose way of life thus obtained pontifical authorization was Francis of Assisi (b. 1181, d. 1226). Son of a well-to-do Italian merchant, he had renounced his inheritance, family, and friends to embrace, in the most literal sense, a life of poverty. Only by being poor, he felt, could he truly follow Christ or reach the hearts and souls of His

[4] Quotations from J. P. Migne, ed., *Patrologia: Series Latina*, CCXVII (Paris, 1889), 190–192.

poor. But this life was not to be sad and morbid. Francis had been a gay young blade in the society of his native town. He was no less gay as a friar. He took great joy in the society of the companions who joined him, and in addition he even loved bird and beast. Justly famous is his Sermon to the Birds. "Children" of all ages can thank him for constructing the first Christmas crib. And there is something of contemporary chivalry in Francis' attitude toward his "Lady Poverty." But really to understand Francis the student had best consult the pages of that remarkable book, *The Little Flowers of St. Francis,* a collection of the sayings and doings of the saint and his early companions.

In 1223, Pope Honorius III finally sanctioned the rule for the new order. Although the official title was the Order of Friars Minor (Latin, *frater;* French, *frère*), members soon became known as Franciscans or, from their habit or costume, as Gray Friars. Not only were Franciscans to have no personal possessions whatever, but not even their order was to own property. Rather they were to rely on the charity of the faithful; hence the term "mendicant" or "begging" friars. They soon attained great popularity especially in the congested towns. In fact, as monasticism was associated with the agrarian life of the earlier Middle Ages, so the friars should be thought of in connection with towns. They were not, however, social reformers in the modern sense of that term. Neither Francis nor his followers had any thought of remaking society. Their ideal was religious, to save the souls of the poor and to reach them by breaking down the barrier which wealth and official position so often raised.

After St. Francis' death, when the order had expanded all over Europe and even to Asia, it was found impracticable to keep the Rule in all its original strictness. As a result, property for convents was usually held in trust for the friars by some lay person. Although St. Francis had never taken major orders, many of his followers became priests. Many, too, became scholars and taught at universities. The philosopher St. Bonaventure (b. 1221, d. 1274) and that somewhat outspoken mathematician, linguist, and all-round scholar, Roger Bacon (d. 1294), were both Franciscans. Surpassing other religious orders, Franciscans numbered nearly 100,000 by 1500.

About the time that St. Francis was embarking on his new life, a Spanish canon, named Dominic (b. 1170, d. 1221), undertook with his superior, Bishop Diego of Osma, a preaching mission among the heretics of Languedoc. Out of this grew a society of clerics devoted to preaching and teaching, for Dominic believed that through proper instruction heretics might be reconciled and the faithful strengthened. Like Francis, Dominic went to Rome and received papal authorization. His Rule, an elaboration and extension of the Augustinian Rule for canons, is a remarkable piece of legislation. Each convent under an elected prior is subject to the periodically elected master-general. The system of representation from the various priories to the general chapter of the order may even have influenced contemporary practices in secular government. Dominicans, officially called Friars Preachers, had to be trained, and this training which began in the schools of the order could continue at a university. As might be expected of an order which emphasized study, there have been many celebrated Dominican scholars, of whom Albertus Magnus (d. 1280) and St. Thomas Aquinas (d. 1274) stand out in the thirteenth century. Poverty was a feature of the Dominican life, although it was not the primary ideal that it was for the Franciscans.

Moreover, every observance, for example the chanting of the divine office, was curtailed if a particular mission so required. Because they wore a black cape over a white garment, Dominicans were known as Black Friars.

The example of the Franciscans and Dominicans was followed by others, among them the Carmelites and the Augustinians. In all cases the Rule enjoined some activity outside the cloister or convent. Hence there arose a distinction between friars and monks. Both are of the regular clergy and live under a rule. But the friars are dedicated to an active rather than a cloistered life.

Heresy

Heresy has been a perennial concern of ecclesiastical government. Broadly speaking, there are always two related problems: first, the doctrinal matter of the particular heresy and, second, the disciplinary measures to be taken against heretics. With regard to the first it must be remembered that heresy is not mere criticism of clerical shortcomings. It is a deliberate dissent from the doctrine or beliefs of the church. It involves, therefore, the intellect as well as the will, reason as well as faith. This dissent, it should further be understood, had to come from one who had known the faith. No Jew or Moslem, unless he had been converted and had accepted the church's authority, could be regarded as a heretic. Such people might be subjected to restrictive regulations, might even be the victims of popular intolerance, but they did not fall under the jurisdiction of ecclesiastical courts set up to try heresy cases.

As we have observed, a primary concern in the matter of heresy has been to clarify doctrine. The Nicene Creed, from two councils (Nicaea, 325, and Constantinople, 381), is a case in point. It embodies the classic definition of the doctrine of the Trinity, a definition called forth to combat the several conflicting doctrines of the Trinity then being propagated. Many other examples could be cited during the long course of church history. The major heresies, therefore, have invariably called forth positive and sometimes detailed definitions of doctrines questioned as well as negative condemnation of error. Moreover, it has been the constant conviction of the church that in such clarification divine guidance would protect it from error.

The discipline of heretics is an altogether different problem, and in the course of its history the church has dealt with the matter in various ways. Invariably the means adopted to deal with heretics reflect the temper of the age, and it requires serious mental effort for the modern student to understand the mediaeval attitude. In the religio-political society of those days heresy was tantamount to treason, and its persistence endangered the immortal souls of the faithful. But what is perhaps most difficult for the modern mind to grasp is the mediaeval view that, to those who had been duly baptized into the church, religious belief was not a matter of free individual choice.

In actual dealings with heretics, the church has had two major objectives: first, the conversion of the heretic and, second, the protection of the faithful. Although in the Middle Ages the secular power was ordinarily expected to assist the church in suppressing heresy, the specific means employed varied considerably. In the late twelfth and early thirteenth century there appeared in southern France a heresy which completely baffled the authorities and eventually called forth the drastic procedures collectively called the Inquisition.

This heresy was known as Albigensianism, from the town of Albi where it gained many adherents, or as Catharism.[5] The latter designation follows from the fact that the leaders of the sect were known as the *Perfecti* or the Pure (*Cathari*). Probably of eastern origin, Catharism bore a resemblance to ancient Manichaeism. Matter and flesh—and the propagation thereof—were held to be evil and in the domain of the devil, while only spiritual things mattered in the service of the true God. It followed, accordingly, that the organization of the church and its sacraments were anathema. But equally to be condemned were war and soldiers and judges who gave the death sentence.

The Perfect lived lives of rigorous asceticism and abstained from all flesh food. In extreme cases, doubtless under fear of imminent corporal punishment, they committed suicide. A peculiar feature of Catharism, however, and one undoubtedly responsible for its spread, was the provision whereby the ordinary believer might live a fairly normal life and simply venerate the Perfect.

By the time of Innocent III (1198–1216), Languedoc was a hotbed of Catharism. It was, in those days, a prosperous, highly cultured, even sophisticated region, and many adherents probably saw in Catharism a criticism of a locally corrupt ecclesiastical organization or, perhaps, an opportunity to appropriate church property. Indeed, Innocent frankly admitted that the southern French clergy gave ample provocation. Moreover, the ordinary means of handling heresy—

[5] A somewhat smaller sect known as Waldensian, founded by Peter Waldo, began as a movement in protest against clerical corruption. When later they adopted heretical doctrines, they were condemned. Many were suppressed along with the Albigensians, but a few persisted and have survived to the present mainly in the Piedmont region.

episcopal courts, preaching, and so forth—failed, especially as various magnates either espoused Catharism or, like Count Raymond VI of Toulouse, refused to aid in apprehending heretics.

Accordingly the pope resorted to an exceptional measure, the crusade. Knights from northern France were summoned to discipline Languedoc. Those who responded were eminently successful in conquering parts of southern France. In fact, Innocent, himself aghast at the fury of the war, intervened to effect some sort of equitable settlement for Count Raymond. Heresy, however, persisted and, it will be recalled, became a major subject for discussion at the Fourth Lateran Council (1215), which promulgated a declaration of faith directed principally against that evil. Even this did not solve the problem, and it remained for Gregory IX (1227–1241), and certain of his successors, to develop special tribunals for trying cases of heresy which came to be known as the Inquisition.

Presiding over such a court was a specially appointed judge or inquisitor, usually a friar. Although he was expressly instructed to assist the local bishop, the latter's role diminished in the course of time. Thus the Inquisition was really a kind of papal tribunal operating locally.

The inquisitor's purpose in any district where the court sat was first to determine which persons were heretics. In short, as the name implies, he was holding an inquiry or inquest. Those formally accused were neither allowed legal counsel nor permitted to know the name of the witness who had given testimony against them. This latter provision, which was later to call forth severe censure, was deemed necessary at the time to protect the witness against revenge by the accused or his supporters; it was, however, modified in a manner intended to protect innocent persons against malicious denunciation by false witnesses. Anyone accused of heresy was allowed to name personal enemies likely to testify dishonestly against him. If by this method he succeeded in identifying any of the actual witnesses in the case, their testimony was deleted. It was not until the mid-thirteenth century that torture was introduced to the procedure of inquest and then only under strict regulation.

The next function of the court was to discipline those heretics whose guilt was proven or admitted and who recanted. Various penances, both moderate and severe, were given. Refusal to recant or lapse after recantation meant death by burning, carried out by the secular authorities. The sentence of death, it should be emphasized, was a confession of failure; the court had not succeeded in its primary purpose of converting the heretic. Only because the persistence of heresy endangered the immortal souls of others was the recalcitrant heretic punished; and in the thirteenth century, it should be added, death sentences were necessary in but a small percentage of the total cases tried.

According to modern standards of legal practice, the papal inquisition was a grim and arbitrary tribunal. Judged by thirteenth-century criteria, it was average. Torture, for example, was included in the Sicilian code of the Emperor Frederick II, usually regarded as an enlightened ruler. The Inquisition seems not to have scandalized public opinion in those days; and its effectiveness is attested by the disappearance of Catharism in southern France. Indeed, until the later Middle Ages it was rarely used outside of Languedoc, the area of the Albigensian heresy.

The Church and Mediaeval Culture

The preceding discussion has described the church as an institution and considered some ways in which that institution functioned. The picture would not be complete, however, without some reference to the role of the church in the mediaeval revival of learning. Mediaeval culture—that is, art, literature, and formal learning—was not, it is true, exclusively religious. Nevertheless, the church was vitally concerned with all these matters.

In the early Middle Ages, formal learning had been divided into the traditional seven liberal arts: the trivium, which included grammar, rhetoric, and logic, and the quadrivium, which embraced arithmetic, geometry, astronomy, and music. In the twelfth century, grammar and rhetoric provided the groundwork for a considerable skill in Latin style, poetic as well as prose, and a wide acquaintance with classical literature. In fact, twelfth-century humanism, that is to say, the love of classical literature, paved the way for its somewhat more pagan and more illustrious counterpart of the Renaissance. The general broadening and deepening of interest in this and other fields of knowledge has led to the designation "renaissance of the twelfth century." It was, indeed, a period of marked intellectual competence in various fields. Its prevailing humanism gave way to the enthusiasm for philosophy and theology which characterized the thirteenth century.

Logic and philosophy received a tremendous impetus, during the second half of the twelfth century, as a consequence of the recovery, largely through contacts with Moslem scholars, of those works of Aristotle which had not been available before. Philosophy flourished in the thirteenth century, and because it was associated with the schools at Paris and elsewhere, it has been called scholastic philosophy.

Logic and philosophy provided the underpinning, the indispensable instrument, for a scientific study of theology which the age regarded as the "queen of the sciences." It was the contention of mediaeval theologians that man could by his intellect, unaided by divine revelation, demonstrate the existence of God and know something of His attributes and His relation to the created world and man. Revealed doctrine, the Trinity for example, could not, it was held, be proven. But such articles of faith must be clearly defined to guard against error, and they could be made understandable, at least in part, to man's intellect. Religious faith, therefore, by no means precluded the use of reason; and philosophy was the instrument of the rationalizing process. In short, logic, as also grammar and rhetoric, would have been considered an intensely practical subject.

Three subjects which the twentieth century might also regard as practical and which the mediaeval revival of learning furthered were mathematics, medicine, and law. Clerics as well as laymen studied all of these subjects. Robert Grosseteste (d. 1253), bishop of Lincoln and sometime chancellor of Oxford, and his celebrated pupil Roger Bacon were among the prominent mathematicians of their day. For any ecclesiastic in an administrative post, knowledge of the law, both civil and canon, was indispensable. There were innumerable dealings between churchmen and laymen, and many of the former still served as officials in government. Not only was canon law essential to ecclesiastical government; its wide jurisdiction made it a useful if not necessary adjunct to the equipment of a secular lawyer.

As the study of logic and philosophy profited by the recovery of the complete Aristotle, so law gained by the rediscovery of the Justinian Code. Early in the twelfth century a legal scholar, named Irnerius, was lecturing and making comments on the *Digest* at Bologna in northern Italy. The study of civil law expanded rapidly, not only at Bologna, but at other centers of learning in southern Europe. And, as was remarked above, it was in the middle of the twelfth century that Gratian produced his treatise on canon law and in the thirteenth that Gregory IX and other popes added their collections of decretals.

Learning depends on students and teachers, and toward the end of the twelfth century the rapidly increasing number of these caused the development of institutions which they called *studia generalia* and which we call universities. Most mediaeval universities grew out of already existing schools in the larger towns. When these schools were church schools, as most of them were, their prominence represents a passing of the primacy in learning from the regular to the secular clergy. Paris is a good example. For decades students had been attracted to the cathedral school of Notre Dame and neighboring institutions by such distinguished teachers as William of Champeaux (d. 1121), Peter Abelard (d. 1142), and others. Taking a leaf from the book of contemporary craftsmen, they formed a guild of students in arts whose "graduates" were masters. Bachelors, a term borrowed from chivalry, were those who had taken an important step or *gradus* (hence "degree") toward becoming masters. As numbers continued to increase, divisions were made into what the mediaeval students called "nations," a term loosely used to classify scholars from various parts of Europe. Each nation elected a representative called the proctor, and the proctors chose a rector who headed the entire organization. Higher "faculties," as they were called, such as canon law and theology, also formed guilds headed by "deans." Thus the academic community at Paris became a federation of guilds. It was the term then commonly employed for guild, *universitas*, which survived and eventually replaced the earlier term *studium generale* as the accepted name for these corporate bodies of students and teachers which have survived to the present day.

It is evident that authorities both ecclesiastical and lay held this new company of scholars in high esteem, for Paris soon received privileges and exemptions from the king of France and from the papacy. In the first part of the thirteenth century it became a virtually autonomous organization, free of immediate episcopal and royal jurisdiction. Shortly, colleges which served as lodgings for students were endowed by generous benefactors. The first such foundation, the gift of Robert de Sorbon, was intended for impecunious scholars in theology. Others followed, and in the course of time colleges became places of teaching and learning as well as of residence.

What was to develop later into a college system is especially associated with the English *studia*, Oxford and Cambridge, where many of the mediaeval establishments remain to this day. Oxford, which was renowned in the thirteenth century for its mathematics, expanded from modest origins, partly as a consequence of an exodus of English scholars from Paris. Cambridge seems to have been an offshoot of Oxford. At any rate, Paris may truly be called the "mother of universities," since the Paris *studium* was the model for many similar institutions in the northern part of Europe.

Most south European universities conformed to the model

of Bologna, which developed into a celebrated institution at about the same time as Paris. Originating, it seems, partly out of very old lay schools of rhetoric and law, partly out of the cathedral school, and partly from monastic establishments, Bologna won renown as a school of law, both civil and canon, and, later, of medicine. Moreover, it was somewhat more lay in character than was Paris and attracted more mature students, men who, in many cases, already had considerable experience and who wanted additional practical training. At Bologna, it was the students who formed the guild (*universitas*) and through this organization controlled their teachers and dictated to the town.

To follow the expansion of the university movement in the Middle Ages, would be quite impossible here. Even before 1300 what had been accomplished at Paris and Bologna was imitated widely. The English foundations have already been mentioned. About 1220 a *studium generale* developed at Salamanca in Spain. There were others in Italy, and in 1347 the Holy Roman Empire had its first university at Prague. Advanced academic training was now an accepted feature of European life and an avenue for advancement in ecclesiastical and professional careers.

Literature and Art

Although the church fostered education from the elementary school in parish and monastery to the university, its connection with literature is less evident. Of course, a large amount of mediaeval literature in Latin, both prose and poetry, was religious. Even the humorous and satirical verse of the *Goliardi*, a kind of informal fraternity of students who journeyed from one school to another, gives ample evidence that the composers were trained in religion and theology. Although much of the popular literature produced in vernacular languages was not religious in spirit, it often contains religious vocabulary and references. Some of the *chansons de geste*, especially the Carolingian cycle of romances in old French of which the *Song of Roland* is the best known, are thought to have developed with the pilgrim movement. Apparently Cluny, which so actively promoted pilgrimage, exploited the Roland story in the journey to Santiago de Compostela. Early forms of the drama can also be traced back to the church, either to the "dramatization" of sections of the liturgy or to religious pageants or representations, sometimes also called miracle plays, performed or sponsored by the guilds. These few examples may serve to demonstrate some of the connections between mediaeval religion and literature.

The connection between art and religion in the Middle Ages is abundantly clear. Although miniaturists, goldsmiths, jewelers, sculptors, and architects worked for nobles and merchants as well as for bishops and abbots, much of the most exquisite craftsmanship went into the building and decorating of churches and the production of ecclesiastical furnishings. The art of illumination, that is, the illustration of manuscripts, usually with intricate detail requiring fine pen or brush, is a noteworthy achievement of the mediaeval centuries.

Sculptors and architects were in great demand by the church, especially after the tenth century. Some of the craftsmen were monks whose labors went into the adornment of their own monasteries. Others were members of masons' guilds. Although we know the names of some mediaeval architects and although some treatises on building and allied subjects appeared, many designers and craftsmen remain anonymous.

There is one feature of mediaeval art which expressed the religious feeling of an entire community. A mediaeval cathedral was usually begun at the instigation of a bishop, but it could be completed only with the assistance of his congregation. Masons and stoneworkers primarily, but also all craftsmen shared in the work. Many a stained glass window commemorates the guild by which it was donated. In some instances the people formed religious associations to assist in the building.

For who ever saw, who ever heard, in all the generations past, that kings, princes, mighty men of this world, puffed up with honors and riches, men and women of noble birth, should bind bridles upon their proud and swollen necks and submit them to wagons which, after the fashion of brute beasts, they dragged with their loads of wine, corn, oil, lime, stones, beams, and other things necessary to sustain life or to build churches, even to Christ's abode? [6]

The highly significant technical and aesthetic contributions of mediaeval architecture to the history of stone construction are not directly relevant here, but no discussion of the mediaeval church would be complete if it did not point out that a great cathedral and, on a smaller scale, even a parish church may be regarded as a summary and synthesis of mediaeval life. The religious devotion of a community, here directed by its bishop, provided the impetus. The most highly developed skills were required—mathematical knowledge, practical experience in stonework, glasscutting

[6] Quotation from a letter of Abbot Haimon in G. G. Coulton, *Life in the Middle Ages*, II (Cambridge, Eng., 1931), 19.

and coloring, the intricate interbalancing of lead, glass, and stone, ironworking, the art of the sculptor, and, above all, a sense of design. Windows and statues reflected the world of nature, of science, and of religion. There are birds and flowers as well as grotesques, angels as well as devils, pagan philosophers as well as Christian theologians, kings and princes as well as God enthroned and surrounded by his saints.

Lest this brief excursion into mediaeval culture seem merely a digression, it may be well to emphasize that artists, scholars, and churchmen believed that society should be an integrated thing and that all human endeavor should be informed by charity—the love of God—and directed toward the attainment of man's supernatural and eternal destiny. Two masterpieces produced in the high Middle Ages preeminently illustrate this view of life. One was the *Summa theologica* of St. Thomas Aquinas (d. 1274), who was, as remarked earlier, a learned Dominican friar, lecturer at Paris, inspired religious poet, and exceptionally brilliant student of philosophy and theology. In various works and particularly in this monumental treatise which he appropriately entitled "the whole," Thomas drew on all the sources of knowledge available to him, Greek, Hebrew, Moslem, Christian. The result is a masterly synthesis which includes not only theology in the narrow sense, but an analysis of man and his attributes—what would today be called psychology—as well as philosophy and metaphysics. Predominantly Aristotelian in its rational underpinning, it ranks as one of the great works of the human mind.

The other masterpiece was the *Divine Comedy* of Dante Alighieri (d. 1321). Writing in the now well-developed Italian vernacular, the *dolce stil nuovo*, this most celebrated of poets recounts a "vision" in which he is taken on a journey through Hell, Purgatory, and Heaven. The poem is an allegorical history of Dante's own soul, of his turning from misguided ways to the true faith and the virtuous life. But the poet also points a moral. In his vivid portrayal of the punishments of the damned and in the deeply philosophical and inspired passages about the souls which are saved, Dante dramatizes the hideousness of sin and the rewards of the blest.

Dante's choice of examples reflects much of his own unhappiness, his exile from his beloved Florence and his sorrow over Italy divided and at war, his sense of outrage at Philip IV's "capture" of the papacy, his abiding belief in the ideal world state. He was also a fearless critic of those clergy who disgraced the church he loved, and there was a place for sinful popes in Hell. In many ways Dante is a unique phenomenon. But his genius is clearly mediaeval and Christian.

CHAPTER IV

The Popes and Political Authority

IN ALL periods of history the church has had to deal with temporal rulers. Even our modern secular age has its problems of church and state. The Middle Ages were no exception, although the political atmosphere in which these relations and, unfortunately, often controversies took place was very different from our own. Difficulties appeared on every level of the ecclesiastical and governmental hierarchies. The investiture dispute, for example, involved not only popes, but many bishops and, in England, the archbishop of Canterbury.

It was also an archbishop of Canterbury, Thomas Becket, who challenged King Henry II (1154–1189) on a matter of English judicial practice. Should clerics found guilty of crime in ecclesiastical courts be punished—a second time, Becket claimed—by secular judges? This famous controversy was especially noteworthy in that it resulted in the archbishop's exile and later martyrdom.[1] Because of widespread indignation at Becket's murder, the English government was, for a time, forced to moderate its demands. The Becket-Henry II quarrel might further be emphasized as an instance of a kind of adjustment which more and more

[1] Sidney Painter, *The Rise of the Feudal Monarchies* (Ithaca, N.Y., 1951), pp. 62 ff.

became necessary as government gained competence and effectiveness. Once a monarchy such as the English extended and improved its judicial procedures, the problem of its jurisdiction over clergy was bound to arise.

A comparable problem arose in the financial realm of government. Should clergy be taxed by kings? Students of French history will remember that King Philip IV (1285–1314) said yes and Pope Boniface VIII (1294–1303) said no. This most spectacular of church-government controversies occurred at the close of the high Middle Ages. Moreover, it involved the papacy, and the papacy presents a special problem which it will be well to elucidate first.

There are two aspects of the papal political program in the Middle Ages. The first, and by far the most easily understood, is the maintenance and government of the papal lands in central Italy. The second, the relations between popes and secular rulers, can be properly understood only against the background of contemporary events and ideas. It will be appropriate, therefore, to consider the papal states at this point.

The Papal States

When the papacy and the Italian government signed the Lateran Treaty in 1929, they were endeavoring to settle in modern terms a question which is as old as the church. For what is known as the Roman Question was raised as soon as the church, emerging from the catacombs, began to take shape as a world-wide organization. Reduced to its essentials, the question is simply one of insistence by the popes upon a territorial state of sufficient size to guarantee political independence for the papacy so that the unhindered administration of the universal church would be assured. The manner of achieving this independence has varied with the political vicissitudes of the Italian peninsula and with changing conceptions of sovereignty. The actual boundaries of the papal state have been the cause of numerous controversies. The principle of territorial independence, however, gradually clarified during the early Middle Ages, has never ceased to be a vital factor in papal policies.

The nucleus of the papal lands was an aggregation of donations dating from the early days of Christianity, widely scattered, but mostly in the vicinity of Rome. Together they came to be known as the Patrimony of St. Peter, a term later used to designate the southwestern portion of the states of the church including Rome. Other gifts followed. In 756, for example, the Frankish ruler Pepin, after defeating the Lombards in north Italy, rescued a large section of former imperial territory, including the region around Ravenna, but instead of restoring it to the emperor at Constantinople, entrusted it to the pope. Subsequent additions which included the duchy of Spoleto (Umbria), the march of Ancona, and southern Tuscany rounded out the traditional papal states in central Italy. An irregular territory with constantly fluctuating boundaries which few mediaeval popes could maintain intact, it stretched, at least in theory, from the River Adige on the northeast to the Garigliano south of Rome.

Until the fifth century the papal possession of land was primarily a matter of property ownership. With the disappearance of the western Roman Empire and the consequent absence of any effective central government, there arose a new and more significant question of political jurisdiction. As imperial authority, now centered in Constantinople, became less and less effective in Italy, the popes were forced to provide for the administration of their lands. For a time in the ninth century Charlemagne (d. 814) restored imperial authority over northern and central Italy. But the political center of gravity of his authority was the Frankish empire of the West, not Constantinople. Moreover, Carolingian privileges in Rome soon became illusory as a consequence of the collapse of the Frankish empire during the ninth century. There followed a kind of anarchy as the military aristocracy in and about Rome, a semibrigand landowning nobility, quick to sense the greater temporal significance of papal power, sought to usurp the authority of their lord through control of the papal office. The same sort of thing was happening to many bishoprics throughout Christendom, but the loss of prestige by the Roman see was of deeper significance.

This was the unhappy situation when the German King Otto I (936–973) and his successors renewed the Carolingian pretensions to power in Italy. Benevolent as this German tutelage was, it presupposed a control which the church of the Cluny era found intolerable. In fact, it was in part against this imperial encroachment on the Holy See that the decree of 1059 on papal elections was directed.

In governing the papal states of central Italy, the popes experienced all the problems which any monarch of the day faced. In addition, their preoccupation with ecclesiastical matters undoubtedly accentuated the defects of administration common to every mediaeval state. In the high Middle Ages the communal movement was added to the perennial problem of a turbulent nobility.

Although the dependent towns were expected to contribute to defense and the feudal nobility were theoretically the clergy's army, the chronic instability of Rome and the papal territory precluded any very effective military force. Pope Leo IX (1049–1054), despite severe criticism, led a kind of holy war against the Normans of southern Italy. Later the Norman rulers became papal vassals and "rescued" Gregory VII from the Emperor Henry IV. Local princes outside the papal states sometimes lent their aid. On certain occasions in the twelfth and thirteenth centuries, the Lombard cities, similarly menaced by the Hohenstaufen German emperors, proved to be valuable allies. Finally, especially in the early thirteenth century, defense of the papal lands was designated a crusade and merged in the larger designs of the popes. Thus the diplomacy of the papal states acquired a broadly European significance.

An especially difficult problem was the government of Rome itself. Mediaeval Rome was but a shadow of the city of the Caesars. Barbarian attacks and the sieges of the sixth century had badly battered the once proud metropolis. With aqueducts cut, the city of the seven hills was a thing of the past, and the population dwindled to a paltry few thousand composed of a decadent military aristocracy, the clergy, and an indigent populace. In the ninth century Saracen raids forced Pope Leo IV to enclose Vatican hill with fortifications. Separate from the rest of the town and thenceforth known as the Leonine city, it contained St. Peter's and the formidable castle of St. Angelo, formerly the tomb of the Emperor Hadrian. In the feudal age unruly nobles raised their own private towers. Ancient ruins—even the famous Coliseum—were made over into strongholds or their marble blocks quarried out for use in new buildings. Churches, monasteries, and private dwellings were fortified.

Ruins, symbols of ancient glory, were lost amid signs of feudal confusion—such was the strange aspect of the city of the popes.

The decree of 1059 had restored the election of the popes to the clergy, but had by no means removed the baneful influence of noble factions on the temporal administration of the city. The situation was further complicated by the appearance of a popular democratic element which, supported by many of the lesser nobles, was ready at the behest of any demagogue to proclaim its independence of both pope and aristocracy. Disorders and insurrections were not uncommon. Moreover, the mediaeval inhabitants of the eternal city fancied themselves the political descendants of ancient Romans. In 1144, for example, Pope Eugenius III was compelled to recognize a "senate." In 1188 a charter was drawn up in the name of the *Senatus populusque Romanus* and was dated not from the year of the reigning pontiff, but "from the forty-fourth year of the institution of the senate at the capitol." Thus the insignia of a once mighty empire adorned a mediaeval commune of a few thousand souls.

A semblance of order was obtained during the pontificate of Innocent III. Innocent's diplomacy, his generosity, and his charity, combined with the Romans' realization that the pope's presence was profitable to them, eventually produced a working agreement. The restoration of papal supremacy throughout Europe brought a stream of suitors, pilgrims, and ecclesiastics from all over the world. Supplying the needs of these people was an occupation far too remunerative to endanger by political wrangling. Innocent also won over many citizens by his encouragement of merchants, by providing alms for the poor, and especially by founding a hospital, later famous as the Hospital of the Holy Spirit, to which no one was denied entrance. He was also more successful than most popes in the administration of the papal states.

Such was the "Roman Question" of the Middle Ages—the establishment of an independent papal state and its defense against usurpation from within and encroachment from without. Defense against invasion became a factor in the papacy's relations with the rulers of Europe, in particular the Holy Roman Emperors, and will be considered further in the following pages.

The Relations between the Popes and the Kingdoms of Europe

In governing Rome and the papal states, the popes employed a direct political authority that can properly be called temporal power. The influence which some popes exercised over secular rulers is an entirely different matter. Actually this papal "intervention" in the affairs of kingdoms is a temporary development and peculiar to the high Middle Ages. Broadly speaking, it resulted from the contemporary interpenetration of things religious and things secular.

Centuries of what has been aptly described as the "secularization of politics" have familiarized the modern world with the idea of an autonomous sovereign state without religious affiliation. But this modern conception of the state as an autonomous political entity, sovereign within its boundaries, scarcely existed in the feudal world of the Middle Ages. Further, the idea of a "church" as an organization apart from the rest of organized society was foreign to the mediaeval mind.

There existed also, especially during the early Middle Ages, a tradition of Roman political unity. This was an idealized concept that the world—or at least Christian Europe—should be politically a unit as it once had been. A powerful tradition, it stood out even in the darkest ages as an ideal which, although never realized, was never abandoned. This ideal was, for example, partly responsible for the persistence in the West of the title Holy Roman Emperor and its assumption by the kings of Germany, although actually this so-called Holy Roman Empire was no more centralized than other European states. Furthermore, on the tradition of Roman political unity had been engrafted the idea of a Christian universalism which the mediaeval mind identified with the "City of God" of St. Augustine.

St. Augustine, it will be remembered, wrote his great *De Civitate Dei* to answer the pagan charge that desertion of the ancient gods was responsible for the "fall"—or at least the sack—of Rome in 410. From this supernatural view of history, early mediaeval thinkers apparently derived their ideal of a religio-political world state as the earthly counterpart of the "City of God." This Augustinian tradition, or political Augustinianism, as it has sometimes been called, conceived of a single unified Christian society which under God had two heads, the pope and the king. There were not two separate societies composed of those in the church and those in the state, because each was coterminous with the other, each included the other. Precisely the same people who were in the church were in the state.

The purpose of this unified Christian society which the Augustinian tradition presented was both religious and secular. It must not only bear witness to Christian revelation and provide for the proper worship of God. It must also serve the ends of justice. It is not surprising, therefore, to find frequent references to the essentially religious character of kingship. Anointed by the priest, he is the chosen defender of the faith, whose duty it is to co-operate in the work of saving souls. Moreover, there were times, for example during the reign of Charlemagne, when the emperor actually assumed spiritual authority. It was the emperor who was called the "vicar of God." A large number of Charlemagne's laws dealt with purely religious matters. In the ninth century, therefore, the unified Christian society was dominated by the emperor, a quasi-religious figure who regarded himself, and acted as, superior in both spirituals and temporals. The distinction so familiar to modern times was completely absent. For a time, at least, the temporal seemed to be the directing force.

With one or two exceptions this temporal hegemony continued to be exercised in varying degrees by many of Charlemagne's successors down to the eleventh century. Gradually thereafter the roles were reversed. Following the recovery of the church during the Cluny period and as a consequence of such controversies as that over lay investiture and the long struggle between the Holy Roman Emperor Frederick Barbarossa and Pope Alexander III, the ecclesiastical rather than the secular tended to dominate.[2] Each viewpoint had its advocates. Political theorists who sought to exalt imperial dignity were opposed by canonists and theologians who more precisely defined the papal position. Both profited immensely by the contemporary legal revival. In the case of the papacy, it is most important to note, a reasonably clear policy and objective developed in the late twelfth and early thirteenth century.

In addition to the customary insistence on unhindered

[2] On Frederick Barbarossa, see Painter, *The Rise of the Feudal Monarchies*, pp. 108 ff.

supervision over the clergy everywhere, certain popes made a valiant attempt to attain peace and justice in Christendom by securing the universal recognition of papal political over-lordship. This conception, hardly developed in the eleventh and early twelfth centuries, was clearly enunciated and nearly realized by the lawyer-popes of the thirteenth century. It implied a kind of union of European states under papal supervision. Accordingly, although the thirteenth-century popes claimed no direct temporal authority outside the papal states, they did attempt to form a sort of federation of kingdoms under papal suzerainty. The primary purpose of this union was a peaceful Christendom conducive to the spiritual and moral welfare of all. But there is no doubt that many popes also hoped that, thus united, Christendom could successfully defend itself against the ever-present Moslem menace and recover Jerusalem. It should be added that this feature of papal policy, the political union of Christendom, is peculiar to the Middle Ages, indeed to the thirteenth century. It was the result partly of contemporary political conditions and partly of the political Augustinianism characteristic of the age.

Papal political action, therefore, was supposed always to have an implicit religious purpose. Sometimes religious aims seem obscured by political methods and consequences. Some popes undoubtedly were less able to maintain a personal detachment than were others. We are not, however, dealing here with a contest for political supremacy, but with an attempt to secure religious ends by means which today we would call political.

The Politics and Diplomacy of Pope Innocent III

It was during the pontificate of Innocent III that the papal temporal pre-eminence reached its height. Never were conditions so ripe for the exercise of some such power as he claimed, and no pope before or since so nearly succeeded in making effective the supremacy of the Holy See over the princes of Europe. Innocent was not an innovator. He followed in the footsteps of his predecessors. But he was gifted with an eloquence and a diplomatic skill which gave a real distinction to his words as well as to his actions.

In virtue of the pope's plenitude of power, Innocent claimed an almost limitless jurisdiction. On one occasion, in comparing the spiritual and temporal authorities, he used the analogy of the sun and the moon. Yet in action he was more circumspect and, as a good lawyer, moved only when sound precedent so indicated. Innocent was, however, no rigid doctrinaire. In applying his conception of pontifical power to the everyday affairs of Europe, he displayed the diplomat's ability to compromise as well as the canonist's knowledge of law.

To recount Innocent III's political career adequately is impossible here. The outstanding developments, therefore, will serve as illustrations. In the Holy Roman Empire, Innocent's conception of papal pre-eminence is particularly well exemplified. As his predecessors before him, he claimed special juridical rights within the empire. These rights were not guaranteed by any feudal contract; nor were they, in the pope's view, based on any general theory of papal temporal overlordship. Rather they were grounded on a traditional relationship dating from the early Middle Ages. Innocent asserted that the papal coronation of Charlemagne in 800 amounted to a "translation" of power from Byzantium to the West by the authority of the papacy. Papal coronation, therefore, was not a mere ceremony, but a formal investiture of imperial power. To the princes belonged the right to elect the emperor, but the election must be confirmed by the pope, who was sole arbiter in cases of dispute. The actual situation confronting Innocent in the empire required both the statement and the exercise of these powers.

The story of Innocent's intervention in the long civil war precipitated by Henry VI's untimely death belongs essentially to the history of the empire.[3] The important fact here is that the young Frederick II, the pope's ward as king of Sicily and his ultimate candidate for the imperial throne, finally emerged victorious in 1214. Moreover, the new emperor made two significant agreements. First, Frederick agreed that his son, then an infant, should be given Sicily. This, it was hoped, would effectively separate the administration of the southern kingdom from that of the empire. Second, he promised to go on a crusade. Thus Innocent seemed at long last to have protected the church, restored to a war-torn Europe some promise of peace, and provided for the crusade. It is true that his high hopes were not to be fulfilled. But when the pope died in 1216, there was reason for optimism.

Innocent's influence was also felt in other states. He continued the feudal policy already developed by his predecessors. In such kingdoms as England, Portugal, Aragon, Sicily, Hungary, Poland, and certain Balkan states, where a feudal contractual relation with the Holy See existed or

[3] See Painter, *The Rise of the Feudal Monarchies*, pp. 117 ff.

was claimed, he jealously guarded his rights as suzerain and wherever possible protected the rights and interests of his vassals. Never a complete success, the papal feudal policy was, however, typical of the age. At best it could and did provide Rome with financial, moral, and occasionally military support. It also strengthened the hand of many a ruler against his adversaries. But papal vassals were usually irregular in the payment of the required *census* and wavering in their political loyalty.

England, although in some ways an exceptional case, is a useful example. King John, it will be recalled, had opposed the pope's right to appoint to the see of Canterbury. When he finally capitulated after years of excommunication and interdict and accepted Innocent's choice of Stephen Langton, he made over his realm as a fief to the Holy See. Manifestly, the king hoped to win papal support against his enemies. It is true that Innocent annulled Magna Carta shortly after its issuance. Whether the pope did this on feudal grounds is, however, a debatable point; and it has been suggested that he condemned the document as extorted by force and containing provisions incompatible with kingly authority. Whatever the reasons, the pope's condemnation did not, in fact, weaken the barons' case. Moreover, the *census* which was due the Holy See from its English fief was grudgingly and irregularly paid and was abolished by Parliament in 1377.

Innocent was careful to distinguish between the vassal states and those admitting no feudal allegiance. Except for normal action to protect local clerical rights, he intervened in such kingdoms, as he himself said, in cases of grievous sin or where careful investigation convinced him that his interference was legally justified. Thus when princes violated the laws of marriage, the pope was quick to act. León, Castile, and France felt the interdict.

In France, however, his intervention met strong opposition. King Philip Augustus (1180–1223) repudiated his wife, Ingebourg, a Danish princess, and managed to procure an annulment from a council of French bishops and barons. Ingebourg then appealed to Rome, and Celestine III, Innocent's predecessor, took steps to quash the judgment. Since Philip proceeded to marry again, Innocent took up the case upon his accession and laid France under an interdict. Eventually the king submitted, but it was years before Ingebourg was reinstated. Meanwhile Philip dealt arbitrarily with the French clergy. Taxes and feudal service were required in spite of the interdict. Moreover, the pope's attempts to mediate in an Anglo-French quarrel over Normandy were fruitless.

Although, as the cases of France and England indicate— and others could be cited—Innocent's policies did not win universal acceptance, he never tired in the pursuit of his aims. Indeed, he did not hesitate to take up matters of only individual or personal importance provided adequate legal grounds for papal action could be found. More than once he championed the rights of widows and minors.

We have dwelt at some length on Innocent's political activities because this remarkable pope approached more closely than any other the goal of a united Christendom. It is true that after the death of Innocent the young Frederick II betrayed the trust his guardian had placed in him. Notwithstanding, as a modern historian has aptly put it, "the modern student will be amazed to discover how nearly Innocent III succeeded in realizing the utopian ideal of a world-organization based on peace and justice. . . . The fact that he failed is not nearly so significant as the degree of success he achieved in the pursuit of an ideal which was itself nothing less than perfection." [4]

Innocent aimed at an international order based on law. The juristic system which he envisaged would have been built on contemporary feudal, Roman, and canon law. Modern nations might reject the particular juridical basis which Innocent had in mind, but a world order founded on respect for law is still the hope of civilized humanity.

Innocent III's Successors

The century following Innocent's death forms at once an epilogue to his career and a prologue to a new age. His manifold assertions of papal political rights found their way into the collections of decretals and provided his successors with material for even more extensive theocratic claims. In the struggle with the Holy Roman Empire, fortune first favored the imperialists, as the young Frederick II, Innocent's protégé, not only held Sicily and southern Italy, but managed by extensive concessions to maintain peace in Germany. When, in addition, he had subdued northern Italy, an attempt was made to negotiate with the papacy; but Innocent IV, genuinely alarmed, declined to compromise. Indeed, the war against the emperor became a crusade and the customary indulgence was offered to all who participated. In 1250 death robbed Frederick of victory, and three years later Innocent IV was able to return to Rome after an absence of nine years. Although the dispute dragged on for some years and in-

[4] Sidney R. Packard, *Europe and the Church under Innocent III* (The Berkshire Studies in European History; New York, 1927), p. 10.

volved Innocent's successors in new diplomatic entangle-
ments, Frederick's death was the turning point in the
historic struggle of papacy and empire.

It is in estimating the significance of Innocent IV's success
that the historian is forced to recognize not only the culmination of the struggle which began with Gregory VII,
but the appearance of political forces pertaining to a new
era. Innocent explicitly laid claim to supremacy over the
princes of the earth. In fact, his deposition of Frederick II
at the Council of Lyons in 1245 has been cited as one of the
clearest and most typical statements of the principle of papal
temporal overlordship. Yet, except for his triumph over the
empire and his dealings with some of the smaller states, his
claim to political supremacy was unavailing. Nor was this
solely because he was so absorbed in the struggle with Frederick that he was unable to give adequate attention to the
rest of Europe. The fact is that the collapse of the Holy
Roman Empire did not pave the way for the triumph of
that papal universalism of which Innocent III had dreamed.
Instead, there developed a secular particularism of national
monarchies. Nowhere is this more apparent than in Innocent
IV's relations with England and France. Henry III of England and Louis IX of France were both exceptionally pious
rulers. Henry was a papal vassal. Louis was a saint. Yet
neither accepted the full implication of Innocent's theocratic claims. Although Louis promised to protect the pope
if he were attacked in Lyons, he attempted more than once
to mediate in the dispute. Both kings continued to address
Frederick as emperor even after papal deposition.

While national monarchies like England and France
gained strength during the later thirteenth century, papal
political influence waned. The famous controversy between

Pope Boniface VIII and King Philip IV of France, to which we alluded briefly at the commencement of this chapter, represents, therefore, a kind of anticlimax in the mediaeval struggle between ecclesiastical and secular power. Boniface was already an old man when he became pope. Moreover, he had many enemies in Italy, some of whom like the poet Dante regarded him as corrupt and wholly unfit for so exalted an office. Notwithstanding, he was a stalwart defender of the papal position. When the pope forbade rulers to tax the clergy without papal permission, Philip, and also Edward I of England, successfully resisted. For a while Boniface dropped the matter and then, shortly after the turn of the century, reopened it. In addition, he protested an adverse decision against a bishop on the part of a secular court. But Philip had assured himself of popular support by summoning a large representative assembly which proved to be the first Estates General. Thus the celebrated bull, *Unam sanctam*, which re-emphasized papal supremacy, made little impression in France. In fact, shortly afterward Nogaret, one of Philip's henchmen, together with Boniface's Italian enemies stormed the pope's residence at Anagni and arrested him. Shocked by the brutality of the perpetrators of this "terrible day of Anagni," public opinion now began to veer toward the pope. He was accordingly released, only to die a month later.

What is the meaning of this episode? It seems clear that European Christians no longer accepted papal interference in what were now regarded as purely political matters. Although there remained doubt as to precisely what constituted purely political matters, the competence of a monarchy within its frontiers was now a fairly well-established fact. But it seems equally clear that an outrage committed against a pope, however unpopular, was widely resented. This is important. Boniface was not a beloved pope; he was regarded in many quarters as a grasping simonist. He evidently had personal enemies in Italy. Dante, it will be recalled, reserved a place for him in Hell. Yet he was still the vicar of Christ. And Dante also reflected the sense of shock felt at Philip's conduct.

It would appear, therefore, that although political terminology familiar to the twentieth century would not have been understood, men in the later thirteenth century were becoming aware of a distinction between secular and religious authority and were willing to recognize the rights of each in its own sphere. It was to be centuries before this modern—or Roman—conception of sovereignty was to be fully understood. Nevertheless, the world of 1300 was, politically speaking, indeed different from that of 1100 or even 1200.

In conclusion it might be emphasized that the notion of a Europe federated politically under papal suzerainty was, like the crusades, vassalage, chivalry, and such matters, the product of the feudal age and passed as feudalism passed. Certainly it had few advocates in the later Middle Ages, and their voices were raised in vain. In modern times the idea has disappeared.

CHAPTER V

Eastern and Western Christendom

The Period before the Crusades:
The Byzantine Schism

IT WAS remarked earlier in this volume that the church in the eastern or Byzantine parts of the former Roman Empire and in lands like Russia and the Balkans which were affected by Byzantine culture followed a course of history different from that of western Christianity. It would be impossible to relate all that history here. Enough should be said, however, to establish the background for an event which occurred in the year 1054 and which was one of the most unfortunate in the long history of Christianity. Although its significance was not realized at the time, the schism which then developed between Constantinople, the major patriarchate of the East, and Rome has persisted down to the present. As a consequence all the relations between East and West—such developments as crusades and missions, as well as political matters—have been affected by this state of schism.

The term "eastern Christendom" is generally understood to mean that part of the Christian world which at one time fell under the jurisdiction of Constantinople. The patriarchate of Constantinople had not always enjoyed a preeminence in the East. Such venerable sees as Antioch, Jerusalem, and Alexandria had been, in view of their apostolic

traditions, of even greater eminence. With the Moslem conquest their prestige had diminished somewhat while that of
Constantinople, the flourishing metropolis of the Mediterranean world, had risen. Indeed, much earlier, at the second
ecumenical council held at Constantinople in 381, the see
of the "new Rome" had been declared second only to the
original or old Rome.

It should also be noticed that Syria, Palestine, and Egypt
had been the scene of certain heresies which undermined the
unity of the Byzantine church. These all had to do with the
Trinity, or more specifically with the person and nature of
Christ. Nestorians, who held that in Christ were two distinct personalities, the human and the divine, were exceptionally active as missionaries to the East. By the eleventh
century they had become strong in Persia and had even
earlier penetrated central Asia and China. Monophysites,
who believed that Christ possessed only one humano-divine
nature, were the most numerous in the immediate Mediterranean region. In Syria they were called Jacobites. Many
inhabitants of Egypt and Ethiopia and most of the Armenians of Asia Minor and the lower Caucasus were also Monophysites. There were scattered communities of Monothe-
lites—one will in Christ—of whom the Maronites of the
Lebanon mountains were the most prominent. Finally, there
were in all these regions many communities which remained
orthodox. Because of the close association between ortho-
doxy and the imperial government at Constantinople, they
came to be known as Melkites or "king's men" (from *malko*,
king).

The Moslem conquerors of the seventh century did not
alter the religious picture as much as might at first be supposed. Over the years, conversions to Islam took place, but

the usual Moslem policy of tribute instead of conversion made possible the continued existence of oriental Christianity. It is also a well-known fact that the native Christians were the cultural intermediaries between the ancient Hellenistic and oriental civilizations and Islam. There was, however, a cultural change inevitably resulting from life in a Moslem environment. Some oriental Christians, for example, abandoned their native liturgical language and adopted Arabic. It became possible, therefore—and still is—to assist at a Christian religious service in the language of the Koran.

Although orthodox Christianity lost ground to Islam and to heresy in Asia and Africa, it made some gains in eastern Europe. In the ninth century two Greek missionaries, Cyril and Methodius, journeyed to Moravia on the fringes of the East Frankish kingdom. There they worked among the native Slavs, and there they derived from the Greek an alphabet suitable to their speech which came to be known as Cyrillic. Despite objections from neighboring German clergy, Rome authorized the Slavonic liturgy. But the Moravian kingdom, which at one time gave promise of forming the nucleus of a flourishing Slavic state, was eventually overrun in the German eastward expansion. As a consequence Moravia became associated politically with Bohemia in the mediaeval German monarchy and ecclesiastically with Rome. Latin replaced Slavonic as the liturgical language. Yet the work of the two missionaries was not in vain, for the Slavonic liturgy was later adopted by Bulgaria and the Slavic peoples of the Balkan peninsula. In 987 Vladimir, prince of Kiev, accepted the Christian faith and opened the way for Byzantine religious and cultural penetration in Kievan Russia. Mediaeval Russian architecture and iconography are thoroughly Byzantine in their inspiration.

Such was the state of the church around the year 1000. Byzantine Christianity, though depleted by heresy and conquest, had made gains elsewhere. Moreover, it was fully in communion with Rome, which it recognized as the supreme see in Christendom. Why, then, did a break occur within a half century?

To begin with, 1054 was not the first official break between the two sees. We need not here explain all the circumstances, but estrangements had occurred before. Broadly speaking, the differences were cultural, political and jurisdictional, and theological. Ever since early Christian times the two sections of Christendom had vastly different historical experiences. Everyday habits of life diverged as did the liturgical languages, Greek and Latin. Not without reason Byzantines looked upon the West as a collection of semibarbarian kingdoms far beneath them in civilization. They regarded the western Holy Roman Empire as a usurpation. On the other hand, westerners who traveled to Constantinople often misunderstood Byzantine ways. At least one mid-tenth-century ambassador from the western empire, Bishop Liutprand of Cremona, was quite scornful of the Greeks. During the eleventh century a complicating factor was added when Norman knights created a new kingdom of southern Italy and Sicily. A number of formerly Byzantine bishoprics were, as a result, transferred to Roman jurisdiction. There were also jurisdictional disputes over Moravia, Bulgaria, and the western Balkans. But the basic difference was the growing unwillingness of Constantinople to admit Rome's supremacy. In fact, this unwillingness underlay such religious divergences as clerical celibacy, the use of leavened or unleavened bread in the Eucharist, and the adoption by the West of the "filioque" phrase in the

Nicene Creed. This last embodied the western insistence that the Holy Ghost, the third person of the Trinity, proceeded from the Father *and the Son*, not, as the Byzantines held, from the Father alone.

The historic reason why so serious a rift developed in the mid-eleventh century was the transformation in the western church which the preceding pages have described. It was no longer true that Byzantine bishops were culturally superior to their western colleagues. The western church had revived and was led by men of intelligence, character, and ability. In its display of religious energy, it was about to outstrip the older civilization of the eastern Mediterranean, and this, unfortunately, the Byzantines failed to realize.

It was equally unfortunate that among the legates sent by the pope for the purpose of discussing various differences was Cardinal Humbert. Humbert was an extremely able person, intelligent and well trained; but he was hardly the soul of tact. Moreover, he epitomized the youthful, energetic, somewhat intransigent spirit of the western church of the Cluny period. That there is much to be said for this spirit earlier pages have demonstrated. It was to accomplish great things during the twelfth and thirteenth centuries. But it was singularly inappropriate for eleventh-century Constantinople, which still regarded itself as the divinely appointed custodian of all that was best in ancient Christian civilization.

The Byzantine patriarch Cerularius was an ambitious man who had insisted on the supremacy of his see over other eastern patriarchates and was now ready to claim at least equality with Rome. Whether the differences could have been resolved by men possessed of greater diplomatic finesse is a question. At any rate, in 1054 negotiations broke down and each party excommunicated the other, Humbert taking the lead. Although neither included the faithful in the opposing jurisdiction, actually a schism resulted which has to this day proved impossible to repair.

Whatever the ultimate responsibility for the schism of 1054, it was one of the most tragic events in Christian history. Not only was Christianity divided, but a cultural rift tending to separate eastern and western Europe was widened with consequences which can be observed even in modern times.

The Crusades

From the time when they occurred to the present, the crusades have commanded public attention and called forth innumerable chronicles, histories long and short, and even poems. Their place in the historiographical tradition of Europe is thus assured, and the very word crusade has become familiar in our vocabulary. But if historians, mediaeval and modern, have agreed that the crusades were interesting and important, they have differed widely in explaining their origins and interpreting their significance. Indeed, it might be questioned whether they belong in a discussion of the mediaeval church. They were, however, launched originally by the papacy; and the church's role, though it diminished, was never negligible. In this brief account it will be possible only to summarize the more generally accepted conclusions.

First, it is clear that the eight large expeditions from 1096 to the later years of the thirteenth century, as well as the many less important ventures, were occasioned by the political and military successes of Islam. In particular, they were a response to a comparatively new menace presented in the second half of the eleventh century by the Seljuk Turks.

The Seljuks had overrun the Bagdad caliphate and as a consequence of a resounding victory over a Byzantine army at Manzikert in 1071 opened the way to the conquest of Asia Minor. Byzantium had faced Islam across the straits before, but never had it lost the entire hinterland of Asia Minor.

Second, the crusades were made possible by the religious, political, and economic energy so characteristic of the eleventh century. The Cluny reform reached a climax in the second half of the century, and it was not difficult for an ecclesiastically militant church to direct its forces to the military defense of Christendom and the recovery of the Holy City, Jerusalem. Politically and economically, eleventh-century Europe was entering one of those periods of expansion which has characterized its civilization down to modern times. Feudal society was far more dynamic than has commonly been supposed. Men were constantly seeking new areas of cultivation and creating new fiefs. Commerce, which had reached a low point during the Dark Ages, was showing a revival which directly affected and was affected by the expeditions to the eastern Mediterranean. In fact, without the shipping facilities of the Italian merchants the crusades would scarcely have been possible.

These are general considerations, and it is over the relative importance of the more immediate causes of the crusades that historians have tended to differ. One of these was the danger to pilgrims making the journey to Jerusalem. Pilgrimage was a well-established feature of European society; it was a journey of devotion to a holy shrine. At first simply a pious act, pilgrimage had in the course of time been adopted by the church as a form of canonical penance. In the eleventh century there were three shrines of especial appeal: Rome, Santiago de Compostela in Spain, and Jerusalem. Although Jerusalem had long been in Moslem hands, pilgrims had usually enjoyed free access until the coming of the Seljuk Turks. Thereafter, hostility toward pilgrims seems to have been fairly common. To the general objective of opposing Islam, therefore, was added the specific purpose of freeing Jerusalem.

To churchmen and especially to popes in the late eleventh century the Byzantine schism was not the long-standing rift which it appears today. It must have seemed merely the latest in a series of misunderstandings which somehow always were overcome. Whether Urban II actually conceived of the crusade as a possible step toward reconciliation may not be said with certainty. But there is no doubt that he ardently desired a reunion and, independently of the crusade, took steps to heal the breach.

The immediate incentive for the First Crusade was the appearance in 1094 at a council held at Piacenza of envoys sent by the Emperor Alexius Comnenus. These Byzantine ambassadors urgently requested military aid against the Turks. Thus, Pope Urban II was made aware of the danger to Europe and, as we have suggested, may have hoped that western assistance might create a more favorable atmosphere in the Byzantine patriarchate.

At the moment the pope apparently planned only a small expeditionary force. From Piacenza he traveled into southern France; there he interviewed a number of people active in both the Cluny movement and the Spanish reconquest, and his ideas seem to have broadened. At Clermont in 1095 he addressed a vast concourse of people in their native tongue, for he was himself a Frenchman. He made a vigorous appeal to naturally warlike knights to abandon their petty quarrels and join their arms in the common defense of Christendom. He spoke of eastern Christianity in peril. He hinted at material reward in the Biblical "land flowing with milk and honey." Finally, he offered the spiritual reward of a plenary indulgence.[1]

The response was overwhelming, probably far greater than the pope had anticipated. The cry, "God wills it," resounded through the crowd, and those who expected to go were soon wearing the cross over their armor; hence the word crusader. Of the men who took the cross, some, in fact probably most, were moved by sincere religious devotion and planned to return once their mission was accomplished. In others, religious zeal was diluted by a desire to win land and glory in the East. Sheer love of adventure was unquestionably a large factor. Further, part of the response had no military significance whatever. Indeed, the motley band of peasants and riffraff which followed the popular preacher Peter the Hermit or the knight Walter the Penniless was actually an embarrassment. But Urban appointed a legate, Adhemar of Puy, to take charge of the real armies and, considering the individualistic habits of feudal knights, a remarkable organization was effected.

Although no kings joined this first expedition, several prominent magnates, notably Raymond of Toulouse, Hugh of Vermandois, brother of the king of France, Bohemond the Norman from southern Italy, Robert of Flanders, Robert of Normandy, Stephen of Blois, and the Lorrainers Godfrey of Bouillon with his brothers, Eustace and Baldwin. Lesser nobles and ecclesiastics associated themselves with these leaders, the great majority being French or Norman. All converged by different routes on Constantinople.

At Constantinople there was trouble. Although Emperor

[1] Not to be confused with sacramental absolution. See above, pp. 8-9.

Alexius desperately wanted military assistance, he was embarrassed by so many westerners who had to be supplied and fed. Moreover, there soon developed a fundamental divergence of aim. Alexius expected conquered territory, at least as far south as Antioch in Syria, to be returned to the empire. Urban II's precise intentions will probably never be clearly known. Both he and his legate, Adhemar, died before the expedition reached its goal. There is no doubt, however, that most of the western leaders fully intended to carve out territories in the Levant for themselves. Yet the necessity for Byzantine aid was evident to all, and therefore, albeit with reluctance, they took an oath of allegiance to the emperor.

Then followed the crossing of the Bosporus, the capture of Nicaea which, according to agreement, was handed over to the emperor, the arduous but victorious march across Asia Minor, and the entry into Syria by different routes. The great city of Antioch offered stout resistance, but when it finally fell, it was at once appropriated by Bohemond the Norman. The Byzantine claim to this city was to prove a serious cause of contention in the future. The other armies continued the southward march and took Jerusalem on July 15, 1099, amid scenes of bloodshed and rejoicing.

Latin Civilization in the Levant: The Later Crusades

We have dwelt at some length on the First Crusade because in many respects it was unique. At no later date did Christendom show even the semblance of unity, imperfect though it was, which was achieved then. And no other crusade attained its objective. This will appear evident in the brief survey which follows.

After the capture of Jerusalem, a great many crusaders, probably the majority, returned to Europe. They had accomplished what they came to do, and they had fulfilled their vow to visit the Holy Sepulcher, the holiest of shrines. But a substantial number remained in the East and settled down as colonists in an alien land. Four principalities were formed: Jerusalem, first ruled by Godfrey of Bouillon with the modest title Advocate of the Holy Sepulcher, then after 1100 by a succession of kings; the county of Tripoli; the principality of Antioch; and the county of Edessa. The last named, being the most vulnerable to attack, was recaptured by the Moslems in 1144. Jerusalem and most of the surrounding territory was taken by the great Saladin in 1187. The remaining two states, Antioch and Tripoli, survived to the last decade of the thirteenth century.

In each of these states western political and military institutions were superimposed on the native agricultural and commercial life. They were, in short, typically feudal structures with native underpinning. In addition, Italian merchants, especially Genoese and Pisans, were accorded privileges in certain of the ports. Their fleets brought reinforcements and supplies and maintained essential contact with Europe. It is true that crusaders adopted many eastern customs, but they were for the most part such things as food and dress which did not fundamentally alter their western culture. Many learned Arabic and other oriental tongues, but their laws were written in old French and their learning was in Latin. The crusaders' states in the Levant may, therefore, best be understood as experiments in colonization, the first chapter in the long history of Europe overseas.

Although there was no formal political connection between the papacy and the crusaders' states, Rome's solicitude persisted. Popes tirelessly preached crusades long after European princes had lost interest. Rome also bestowed privileges and exemptions on the religio-military orders of Knights Templars and Knights Hospitallers. The former, established initially at the Temple in Jerusalem, was dedicated to the protection of pilgrims. The latter, originally devoted to the care of the sick, later added military functions. Both performed yeoman service in the defense of the crusaders' states, especially in garrisoning the frontier castles.

Papal legates were constantly sent to the East and local bishops attended western councils. There was, indeed, a Latin hierarchy in the East, and the major religious orders soon made their appearance. Churches and parishes were established in converted mosques or in new edifices erected in western style. In short, everything was done to create a normal ecclesiastical situation.

Although all crusades were essentially religious and the First Crusade pre-eminently so, the lay element predominated more and more in later years. The Second Crusade (1148–1149), for example, occasioned by the capture of Edessa in 1144, was authorized by the pope and preached by the great St. Bernard. But it was really managed by King Louis VII of France and Emperor Conrad III of Germany. It was a disappointing failure. Moreover, three decades later that most distinguished Moslem leader, Saladin, had combined Egypt and the Syrian hinterland, thus surrounding the Latin states with a single Moslem power. Profiting cleverly by chronic dissensions among the crusaders, he defeated a Christian army at Hattin and recaptured Jerusalem in 1187.

Once again Rome endeavored to arouse Europe, and with no little success. The Third Crusade (1189–1192) was, however, a lay affair and was led by three kings, Richard the Lion-Hearted of England, Philip Augustus of France, and Frederick Barbarossa, Holy Roman Emperor. Cyprus was captured from Byzantium and the Levantine port of Acre was recovered in 1191, but Jerusalem remained in Moslem hands.

The troops assembled for the Fourth Crusade (1202–1204) began by capturing—largely at Venetian urging—Zara on the Adriatic in Christian Hungary and then (1204) converged on Constantinople. The former diversion resulted from the crusaders' inability to meet the Venetian's fee for transportation with cash; instead they arranged to pay for their passage with this military service. The attack on Constantinople, however, derived in part at least from a desire of some of the leaders to support a pretender to the Byzantine throne. The conquest of the great metropolis of the eastern Mediterranean was, therefore, probably not originally intended. But many of the crusaders and the Venetians profited handsomely. Pope Innocent, who had originally levied contributions to support the crusade, excommunicated the leaders, but, finding himself utterly unable to control their actions, made the best of a bad situation by recognizing a new Latin empire in Constantinople with Latin patriarch and clergy. The consequences of this misdirected crusade were far-reaching. Not only were relations between the eastern and western churches irrevocably injured, but the Byzantine empire was permanently damaged. It maintained a precarious existence in Asia Minor until 1261, when with the aid of Genoa, traditional rival of Venice, the Latin empire was overthrown and Constantinople recovered. Not all former Byzantine territory, however, was restored, and the empire never regained its former prestige. In its weakened state it was a prey to the Moslem invasions of the later Middle Ages.

Innocent continued his efforts, but did not live to see the Fifth Crusade (1218–1221). It was just as well. Although the plan to attack Egypt was sound, the papal legate in charge of the expedition disregarded the advice of lay leaders, and the Christian armies were defeated. The Sixth Crusade (1228–1229) was a distinctly lay affair. The Emperor Frederick II succeeded—he was under excommunication at the time—in arranging a treaty permitting partial control over Jerusalem. This ended in 1244. The last two expeditions which have been designated by number, the Seventh (1248–1250) and the Eighth Crusades (1270), were directed by St. Louis IX of France. Both failed. Finally in 1291 the last Christian territory on the Levantine mainland was taken by the Mamluks of Egypt. For about two centuries a "kingdom of Jerusalem" was maintained in Cyprus, and popes never ceased the attempt to arouse Europe. But Europe was no longer concerned. Even the Ottoman Turk invasion of the Balkans in the fifteenth century failed to elicit any response except from the people immediately affected in eastern Europe. And that was not enough.

The Consequences of the Crusades: Eastern and Western Christendom in the Thirteenth Century

It is not easy to estimate the consequences of the crusades to the church. On the whole, it seems clear that the First Crusade, by establishing the papacy as leader of a great cause, immensely strengthened that institution at a critical period in its history. It is equally clear, however, that no such favorable consequences followed thereafter. In the first place, as we have observed, the movement became at once less papal and more lay in its direction and control. Second, there was failure. An added factor was the increased use of crusades and crusade privileges for European causes. The long intermittent war of reconquest in Spain was a crusade, and there were critical occasions when Rome sought to achieve a united effort by active intervention. Success, for example, crowned Innocent III's efforts when a Christian army drawn from France and the various Spanish states won a striking victory at Las Navas de Tolosa in 1212. There was also the crusade against the Cathari in southern France. But if the former resembled the expeditions to the Orient in being directed against the Moslems and if the latter was religious in origin, Innocent IV's proclamation of a crusade against his Hohenstaufen enemy, Frederick II, seemed to many contemporaries a political move. It is entirely possible that this policy contributed to the loss of support by Europeans for crusades to the East.

This is not the place to discuss the many developments, economic, political, and social, which were directly or indirectly the result of the crusades. What is pertinent to a study of the mediaeval church is the matter of eastern Christendom. It was remarked earlier that Urban II was anxious to end the Byzantine schism and may well have hoped that the crusade would produce a favorable atmosphere. The result was otherwise. Mutual suspicion accentuated by the fundamental divergence of purpose marred the relations between westerners and Byzantines from the first meeting at Constantinople. During the twelfth century there were controversies over Antioch. There were, it is true, a few occasions when a Latin-Byzantine military alliance operated, but nothing tangible was accomplished. Toward the end

of the twelfth century relations deteriorated and were irrep-
arably injured by the Fourth Crusade. Discussions between
eastern and western ecclesiastics proved equally futile. The
last of these in the period here under consideration was at
the Council of Lyons in 1274 under Pope Gregory X (1271–
1276), a man who had been papal legate in the Orient and
was as a result particularly well informed about the entire
situation. The hard-pressed Byzantine emperor, Michael
Paleologus, made a profession of faith; but the church in
Constantinople declined to follow. Thus the Byzantine
schism deepened.

Although failure must be recorded in Romano-Byzantine
relations, there were several notable successes with other
oriental Christians. The establishment of the crusaders' states
provided the first direct contact which the western church
had had with these people since the Arab conquest in the
seventh century. Actually, oriental Christians had become
largely Arabic in culture and without marked sympathy for
the crusaders. And too often the latter regarded their Syrian
confrères with unconcealed contempt. But although local
Latin ecclesiastics sometimes lacked understanding, Rome
generally championed the ancient liturgical customs of any
oriental group which accepted the primacy of the Holy See.
Moreover, as a consequence of an expanding missionary
movement much was learned of the languages and usages of
oriental Christianity.

In the kingdom of Jerusalem the Melkites, or orthodox
Syrian Christians, seem to have accepted the Roman hierarchy. Indeed, it is a question to what degree they had been
affected by the schism of 1054. Their colleagues in Antioch,
on the other hand, remained loyal to Byzantium. Of the
heretical Christians, aside from a few individual Jacobite and

Nestorian bishops and their congregations, the largest gains were made among the Maronites of the Lebanon mountains (1182) and the Armenians. In the thirteenth century King Hayton II of the Armenian kingdom in Cilicia just to the north and west of Antioch entered the western church and became a Franciscan. At the synods of Sis (1307) and Adana (1316), Armenian bishops accepted a formula of reconciliation with the western church. During the fourteenth century Dominicans won over a large group in what is known as Greater Armenia, the region south of the Caucasus. In fact, a native branch of the Dominican order was established. As later events were to prove, however, many Armenians remained hostile to Latin Catholicism. After the Turkish conquests in the later Middle Ages, all but a few of the Armenians reverted to the Monophysite heresy.

The Latin states of Syria and the temporary occupation of Constantinople provided the jumping-off-places for missions deeper in Asia. These were further facilitated by the great expansion of the Mongol empire. Although Genghis Khan and his armies had terrorized Europe in the early decades of the thirteenth century, his successors founded a vast empire which stretched from the borders of Hungary to the Pacific Ocean and adopted an attitude of toleration toward western missionaries and travelers. It was in 1245 that Innocent IV sent out his first missionaries to the Mongols with a threefold aim: to mitigate the Mongol depredations in eastern Europe, to secure an alliance against Islam, and to make conversions. Rumors reached Europe that many Mongol chieftains and their princesses were on the point of embracing Christianity. Although these reports were grossly exaggerated, it remains true that a number of Mongol magnates were Christian and that Nestorian Christianity had expanded in central and eastern Asia with the Mongol conquests.[2] It is also true that the Mongol push southwestward was stopped in Syria in 1260 by the Egyptian Moslems. An alliance between Mongols and western Christians was not, therefore, entirely fantastic.

The first missionary-ambassadors were two Franciscan friars, John of Plano Carpini and Benedict the Pole. They journeyed overland and, after experiencing terrific hardships, reached the capital or camp at Karakorum in Mongolia. Fortunately, although the mission was not successful, John left a remarkably detailed account of his travels. Together with Benedict's shorter story, it is invaluable as the first glimpse by Europeans into central Asia. A decade later another Franciscan, William Rubruk, made a similar journey which he also described in detail.

After the Mongols had founded their capital at Khanbalik (later Peking), Europeans were not slow in making an appearance in China, as the book of Marco Polo testifies (c. 1297). Indeed, one of the most celebrated of all missionaries was the Franciscan John of Montecorvino, who in 1291 set out from Persia for Khanbalik, arrived in 1294 after traversing parts of India, and established a mission in the Mongol capital. He was so successful that in 1307 Pope Clement V created the archdiocese of Khanbalik, probably the largest in the history of the church because it embraced the entire Mongol empire. John was the first incumbent and was consecrated by three bishops whom the pope sent out to

[2] It was also widely held in Europe that a Christian king, Prester John, ruled somewhere in Asia. Marco Polo and others attempted to identify this kingdom. During the fourteenth century it came to be believed that Prester John was an African, presumably an Ethiopian, ruler.

strengthen the Franciscan mission. Two letters John wrote to the pope have survived as evidence of his accomplishments. But others testified to the esteem in which he was held by pagans as well as Christians.

That archbishop, as it pleased God, is lately passed from the world. To his obsequies and to his burial there came a very great multitude of Christian people and of pagans. And these pagans rent their mourning robes as their way is; and these people, Christians and pagans, most devoutly took the garments of the archbishop and kept them with great reverence and for relics. There was he buried with much honor in the fashion of faithful Christians. People still visit the place of his burial with very great devotion.[3]

Meanwhile, Dominican missionaries had been active in the Latin empire of Constantinople, in the Crimea, and in other parts of the Mongol dominions. As we have already mentioned, they were particularly successful in Greater Armenia. In 1318, Pope John XXII withdrew from the province of Khanbalik some of its southern territory and created a new province with Dominican bishops and with archiepiscopal see at Soltania in Persia.

Political upheavals of the fourteenth century, the recovery of the Ming dynasty in China (1368), the conquests of Tamerlane, the advance of Islam in central Asia, and finally the rise of the Ottoman Turks brought a premature end to these far-flung missionary ventures. There had not, in all probability, been many converts, and apparently most of these were from formerly oriental Christian sects. But

[3] Quoted from *The Book of the Estate of the Great Kaan*, tr. in-A. C. Moule, *Christians in China before the Year 1550* (London, 1930), p. 250.

promising beginnings had been made, and it is well to remember that early in the fourteenth century Latin Christianity had reached the Pacific and the Indian oceans.

Conclusion

The preceding chapters have reviewed the development of the church as an institution, and we have seen something of its impact on mediaeval society. Viewing it in this light —as an institution developing within a given period of history—historians generally agree that the mediaeval church reached a climax in such development sometime during the thirteenth century and that there followed a falling off or "decline." To evaluate and explain the growth and expansion of the mediaeval church has been the purpose of this essay; but, except to note the political and economic tensions of the later thirteenth century, no attempt has been made to explain the role of the church in the later Middle Ages.

It is, however, appropriate here to repeat what was said in the introduction—that the institutional history of the church is only part of the story. What is at once less apparent and more important is the church's influence over the lives of individual men and women. To a certain degree we have observed this in the careers of the great. But what of the ordinary person, the knight, the peasant, the merchant, the housewife? Inadequate as our estimate must be, it may nevertheless be worth while to attempt, by way of conclusion, some answer to this question.

To begin with, the cultural atmosphere of the high Middle Ages was definitely religious. Religion permeated learning, art, and literature. Although learning was the privilege of a comparatively few people, art and literature were enjoyed by a much wider and a growing public. There is also ample evidence of popular religious devotion. Books of hours, adaptations of the monastic office, were prepared, sometimes with handsome illustrations, for the laity. Men and women formed religious confraternities, and guilds contributed stained glass windows to the cathedrals. The supernatural was very real. Angels and evil spirits were ever at hand. Men venerated saints and prized their relics. Indeed, the authorities were forced to take action against the traffic in spurious relics. As is evident from the Middle English vocabulary, religious terms, or perversions thereof, became everyday ejaculations or oaths.

Above all, mediaeval man held the Virgin Mary, the Mother of God, in the highest devotion. Countless cathedrals and churches were erected in her honor, and many were the hymns dedicated to her. Recitation of the popular prayer, the "Hail, Mary," with the aid of rosary beads became extremely popular during the Middle Ages. Mary was the "gracious advocate" for sinful souls fearing divine punishment.

If we understand the term in its proper significance, the Middle Ages were religious. This does not mean that mediaeval men and women spent all their hours in prayer or that they took little joy in living. Manifestly, such was not the case; and the exaggerated contrast between mediaeval "otherworldliness" and Renaissance secularism has largely been abandoned. What is true is that mediaeval society accepted the principle that man was destined for another life and that all his actions were potentially significant in shaping his eternal destiny.

Suggestions for Further Reading

THE most useful general studies on the mediaeval church are A. C. Flick, *The Rise of the Medieval Church* (New York, 1909); J. A. Foakes-Jackson, *Introduction to the History of Christianity* (New York, 1921); P. Hughes, *A History of the Church*, Vols. I and II (New York, 1934, 1935); K. S. Latourette, *A History of the Expansion of Christianity*, Vol. II, *The Thousand Years of Uncertainty* (New York, 1938); and D. S. Schaff, *History of the Christian Church*, Vol. V, *The Middle Ages* (New York, 1907). S. Baldwin, *The Organization of Medieval Christianity* (New York, 1929), is a brief treatment.

Students should also consult the appropriate chapters in the *Cambridge Medieval History*, Vols. V and VI (Cambridge, Eng., 1929), and *The Shorter Cambridge Medieval History* (ed. C. W. Previté-Orton, 2 vols., Cambridge, Eng., 1952). For those who read French, the following are especially recommended: A. Fliche, *La Chrétienté médiévale* (Paris, 1929), and the series of volumes in the *Histoire de l'église* edited by A. Fliche and V. Martin. There is also a French translation of G. Schnürer, *Kirche und Kultur im Mittelalter* (*L'Eglise et la civilisation au moyen âge*, 2 vols., Paris, 1933–1935), and an English translation of Vol. I (*Church and Culture in the Middle Ages*), by G. J. Undreiner (Paterson, N.J., 1956). Other works on the relation of the church to mediaeval society are H. Daniel-Rops, *Cathedral and Crusade* (New York, 1957), and C. Dawson, *Religion and the Rise of Western Culture* (New York, 1950; Image Books, 1958).

For the papacy, a good general treatment is W. F. Barry, *The Papal Monarchy from St. Gregory the Great to Boniface VIII* (New York, 1902). H. K. Mann, *The Lives of the Popes in the Middle Ages* (18 vols., London, 1906–1932), is a series of biographies of popes rather than a study of the papacy. W. Ullmann, *The Growth of Papal Government in the Middle Ages* (London, 1955), is one of the best recent studies in English. J. A. Corbett, *The Papacy* (New York, 1956; Anvil Books, 1956), is a collection of documents with useful comments.

See also the following studies of individual popes: L. E. Binns, *Innocent III* (London, 1931); T. S. R. Boase, *Boniface VIII* (London, 1933); J. Clayton, *Innocent III and His Times* (Milwaukee, 1940); A. J. MacDonald, *Hildebrand: A Life of Gregory VII* (London, 1932); S. R. Packard, *Europe and the Church under Innocent III* (New York, 1927); C. Smith, *Innocent III, Church Defender* (New York, 1951).

For the Inquisition, see H. C. Lea, *A History of the Inquisition in the Middle Ages* (3 vols., New York, 1888); A. L. Maycock, *The Inquisition from Its Establishment to the Great Schism* (London, 1931); E. Vacandard, *The Inquisition* (New York, 1924); and A. C. Shannon, *The Popes and Heresy in the Thirteenth Century* (New York, 1949).

On the political theory of papal temporal power, see A. J. and R. W. Carlyle, *A History of Medieval Political Theory in the West* (6 vols., Edinburgh and London, 1903–1936); C. H. McIlwain, *The Growth of Political Thought in the West from the Greeks to the End of the Middle Ages* (New York, 1932); G. Tellenbach, *Church, State, and Society at the Time of the Investiture Contest* (Oxford, 1940); W. Ullmann, *Medieval Papalism: The Political Theories of the Medieval Canonists* (London, 1949).

On the history of monasticism and the friars, see R. F. Bennet, *The Early Dominicans* (Cambridge, Eng., 1927); E. C.

Butler, *Benedictine Monachism* (2d ed.; London, 1924); E. S. Davison, *The Forerunners of St. Francis* (New York, 1926); A. Harnack, *Monasticism* (1901); and H. B. Workman, *The Evolution of the Monastic Ideal* (London, 1913). Somewhat more detailed are G. G. Coulton, *Five Centuries of Religion* (5 vols., Cambridge, Eng., 1923–1936); W. A. Hinnebusch, *The Early English Friars Preachers* (Rome, 1951); and R. M. Huber, *Documented History of the Franciscan Order, 1182–1527* (Milwaukee and Washington, 1944–   ). Outstanding recent works on English monasticism are D. Knowles, *The Monastic Order in England* (Cambridge, Eng., 1940), and *The Religious Orders in England* (Cambridge, Eng., 1948).

The following biographies are also important: J. Chapman, *St. Benedict and the Sixth Century* (London, 1929); F. C. Copleston, *Aquinas* (London, 1955; Penguin Books, 1955); B. S. James, *St. Bernard of Clairvaux* (New York, 1957); B. Jarrett, *Life of St. Dominic* (London, 1924); J. Maritain, *St. Thomas Aquinas* (New York, 1959; Meridian Books, 1958); J. McCann, *St. Benedict and His Times* (New York, 1958; Image Books, 1958); and W. Williams, *St. Bernard of Clairvaux* (Manchester, Eng., 1944). For St. Francis of Assisi, see studies by T. S. R. Boase (1936), Fr. Cuthbert (1913), J. Jorgenson (1912; Image Books, 1955), R. C. Petry (1941), and P. Sabatier (several editions).

Useful short studies on the crusades are E. Barker, *The Crusades* (London, 1925; reprint of an article in the *Encyclopaedia Britannica*); D. C. Munro, *The Kingdom of the Crusaders* (New York, 1935); and R. A. Newhall, *The Crusades* (New York, 1927). A recent excellent treatment is S. Runciman, *A History of the Crusades* (Vols. I and II of a projected three volumes, Cambridge, Eng., 1951–1952). *The First Hundred Years*, Vol. I of *The Pennsylvania History of the Crusades*, ed. K. M. Setton and M. W. Baldwin (Philadelphia, 1955), is the first of a multivolume series. On Byzantine Christendom there is material in the appropriate chapters of N. H. Baynes,

The Byzantine Empire (New York, 1926); N. H. Baynes and H. St. L. B. Moss, *Byzantium* (Oxford, 1948); and S. Runciman, *Byzantine Civilization* (London, 1933; Meridian Books, 1956). C. R. Beazley, *The Dawn of Modern Geography* (3 vols., London, 1897–1906), L. Olschki, *Marco Polo's Precursors* (Baltimore, 1940), and A. C. Moule, *Christians in China before the Year 1550* (London, 1930), will give an introduction to the story of missions to Asia.

The extensive subject of the church and mediaeval culture has been treated, in one or another phase, by a number of excellent studies, among which the following will serve as introduction: Henry Adams, *Mont Saint-Michel and Chartres* (New York, 1913; Anchor Books, 1959); C. G. Crump and E. F. Jacob, *The Legacy of the Middle Ages* (Oxford, 1926, 1932); M. De Wulf, *Philosophy and Civilization in the Middle Ages* (Princeton, 1922); A. Freemantle, *The Age of Belief* (New York, 1954; Mentor Books, 1955) (which contains selections from the writings of the principal medieval philosophers); E. Gilson, *The Spirit of Medieval Philosophy* (New York, 1936); C. H. Haskins, *The Renaissance of the Twelfth Century* (Cambridge, Mass., 1927; Meridian Books, 1957), and *The Rise of Universities* (New York, 1923; Great Seal Books, Ithaca, N.Y., 1957); D. J. B. Hawkins, *A Sketch of Medieval Philosophy* (New York, 1947); G. Leff, *Medieval Thought from Saint Augustine to Ockham* (London, 1958; Penguin Books, 1958); E. Mâle, *Religious Art in France in the XIIIth Century, the Gothic Image* (New York, 1913, 1958; Noonday Press, 1958); C. R. Morey, *Mediaeval Art* (New York, 1942); C. R. Morey, *Christian Art* (New York, 1935; Norton Library paperback, 1958); J. Pijoan, *History of Art*, Vol. II (New York, 1928); H. Rashdall, *The Universities of Europe in the Middle Ages* (3 vols., revised by F. M. Powicke and A. B. Emden, Oxford, 1936); and G. Walsh, *Medieval Humanism* (New York, 1942).

Index